Organic
Fruits and
Vegetables

Organic Fruits and Vegetables

Growing Healthy and Delicious Food at Home

By Teo Gómez
with Quico Barranco

Translated by Elizabeth Watson

Skyhorse Publishing

*"If you want to be happy for a day, drink.
If you want to be happy for a month, travel.
If you want to be happy for a year, get married.
If you want to be happy for life, become a farmer."*

CHINESE PROVERB

* * *

DEDICATED TO SERAFIN SANJUAN AND ALVARO ALTES, PIONEERS OF ECOLOGICAL AGRICULTURE.

Editor's Note: The advice in this book is based on a temperate climate. Refer to your seed packets or a gardening professional if you're located outside temperate zones. Although every effort has been made to ensure that the information in this book was correct at press time, the author and publisher hereby disclaim any liability to any party for any loss, injury, damage, or disruption caused by errors or omissions. Please note that any advice contained herein may not be suitable for every individual.

Original title: TU HUERTO Y JARDÍN ECOLÓGICOS
© 2007 EDITORIAL OCÉANO, S.L.
(BARCELONA, SPAIN)

Photos: Corbis, Getty, Océano archives; Illustrations: Xavier Bou

English translation © 2016 by Skyhorse Publishing

Skyhorse Publishing books may be purchased in bulk at special discounts for sales promotion, corporate gifts, fund-raising, or educational purposes. Special editions can also be created to specifications. For details, contact the Special Sales Department, Skyhorse Publishing, 307 West 36th Street, 11th Floor, New York, NY 10018 or HYPERLINK "mailto:info@skyhorsepublishing.com" info@skyhorsepublishing.com.

Skyhorse® and Skyhorse Publishing® are registered trademarks of Skyhorse Publishing, Inc.®, a Delaware corporation.

Visit our website at www.skyhorsepublishing.com.

10 9 8 7 6 5 4 3 2 1

Library of Congress Cataloging-in-Publication Data is available on file.

Cover design by Qualcom
Cover photo credit Thinkstock

ISBN: 978-1-63450-347-1
Ebook ISBN: 978-1-63450-908-4
Printed in China

Contents

Introduction: Why ecological agriculture?

In a not-so-distant future, producers will have to opt for organic crops, products free from chemicals, in the face of increasing demand.

Any agricultural practice that doesn't contaminate the environment and consumes a reasonable amount of energy—including manual labor, the use of machines, and the consumption of fertilizers—can be considered ecological.

Therefore, ecological agriculture should eliminate as much as possible the use of fertilizers and pesticides on plants. In the case of animals, it should avoid growth regulators in general, including steroids, and the use of medications and dietary supplements.

You could say that the agriculture practiced in ancient times was ecological, since they did not use fertilizers or chemical products to fight plagues or diseases in the plants. However, when we go beyond the regions where agriculture fostered civilizations, it becomes clear that the agriculture that we are going to practice is *more* ecological than that practiced by, for example, the Sumerians.

Agriculture began in the Near East, in the deltas of the Tigris, Euphrates, and Nile rivers. The young land, formed by sedimentary material washed down from the mountains, had an extraordinary yield because it had never been utilized before.

Land formed in this way produces abundant harvests without needing fertilizer for many years, and then begins to lack essential components that have all been absorbed by the plants. In the Nile, the annual floods brought fertile soil from the mountains of Ethiopia and deposited it across the valley, on both sides of the river, renewing the nutrients each year. In Mesopotamia something similar happened, although the expansion of farming into higher areas forced them to fertilize with the manure of livestock in order to use the soil continually. The ingenious irrigation systems of the Sumerians and Babylonians did not account for the fact that when the water evaporated in the channels, the salt stayed behind and accumulated on the surface and, over time, left the land barren.

The myths of industrial agriculture

Agricultural engineers, chemists, and politicians in general defend industrial agriculture as the only option to end world hunger. Why? Because of the scarce yield of organic agriculture, which requires a greater amount of manual labor and produces less.

First myth

Industrial agriculture will produce food for everyone. In poor countries, many farmers have been dispossessed of their lands, from which they obtained subsistence foods, in order to produce industrial foods such as tobacco and cotton, which only benefit landowners and the government. In Latin America and Africa there are still vast expanses of uncultivated land that could feed millions of people. In the Amazon, they transform immense tracts of jungle into poor pasture land to

This windmill is the cleanest way to bring up ground water without polluting the environment. Unfortunately, they have almost completely disappeared from the landscape, to be replaced by electric pumps that depend on the burning of fuel in a power plant.

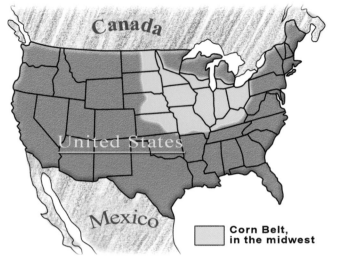

Canada

United States

Mexico

**Corn Belt,
in the midwest**

produce hamburgers destined for North Americans. In many parts of Africa, it would only take some irrigation to convert hundreds of thousands of hectares of arid and unused lands into worthwhile crop land.

Second myth

Industrial foodstuffs are healthy and nutritious. It is enough to just mention the pesticides, insecticides, and genetic modification, which could cause cancer in the long term and which damage the environment.

Third myth

They are cheaper. The social and environmental cost of products created in laboratories is very high, and that's not to mention the dependency created around them. They expel small farmers from their lands, and pollute the atmosphere and soil. It is not true that industrial agriculture produces higher yields, since it has been demonstrated that small parcels cultivated intensely, as is done in Japan and Italy, produce a much higher yield in all aspects. The myth that genetically modified plants are more resistant to disease is also false, since, as we will see, they require specific pesticides and insecticides and make farmers dependent, as well as replacing more flavorful and nutritious species.

In this map, observe the Corn Belt in the Midwestern United States, very rich tracts of land where they have applied the most efficient technology in fertilization and genetic engineering. Government subsidies make the production so inexpensive that corn grown in this way is cheaper on the global market than that grown the traditional way in Mexico, where manual labor is much cheaper. The result is that more and more people are abandoning systems of production that are hundreds of years old, an extraordinary genetic diversity is being lost, and a good part of the farming community is going broke.

The cosmetic value of fruits and vegetables is becoming increasingly more important than other aspects, such as flavor and nutritive value. For this reason they apply harmful wax to oranges, for example.

Mechanization

It is normal to think that the mechanization of agriculture is a notable improvement and should stimulate production. Well, this is a superficial conclusion, and in many cases is the result of propaganda from those who profit from it. It does not benefit the rural community, which ends up in poverty, unemployed, or in the city, but rather the consumer who can squander more. This happens not because the citizens are organized, but because the farmers are not and the corporations are, due to the small size of our country and researchers paid by them. Mechanization must be cut back because it is responsible for rural depopulation, the reduction of the quality of products, and enslavement to the anonymous societies in possession of the technological arsenal. These failures indicate that mechanization is ineffective and uneconomical.

Let's look at a real case: Recently, the University of Florida developed, for mechanical harvest, a salad tomato whose characteristics make it optimal for the harvester: thick lining, hard pulp, and skin that does not break. This is perhaps a little tough for the consumer, but you can't please everyone. The use of this tomato will eliminate thousands of jobs in Florida alone, but in some ways that is an advantage, since machines don't create the same conflicts.

It is designed to be harvested green and ripen while stored by applying ethylene gas. It has been demonstrated that this gas reduces the quantities of vitamins A and C, the flavor, and the consistency in tomatoes, but the South Carolina Agricultural Experiment Station has demonstrated that treating tomatoes with red fluorescent light increases their red color, and the taste and consistency become similar to those ripened on the vine. The University of Ohio confirms that tomatoes peeled chemically with moisturizing agents and caustic lye reduce the work by 75 percent and increase the final output. Did anyone ask what the consumer thinks of this? Is it guaranteed that those who make the machines, control the gas and oil, make the herbicides and fertilizers, process, store, and distribute, will not extort the mechanical grower? And who wants to know what has happened to the vitamins?

The legacy of chemical pesticides left by World War II, selective cross breeding, and cultural improvements increased crop production in California from 60 tons per hectare, to 100. But one enemy emerged: the people. It's an enormous industry that is almost entirely manual. The fluctuation in the workforce was more or less manageable, but the order from Washington was that no more dollars were to leave the country: the migrant workers had to stay in their country. Although the industry did not collapse because it already had machines and the tomato had already been "improved" to suit the use of machines.

At the University of California, Hanna, a geneticist, was looking for a tomato that grew like a conifer, with the fruits on a conical surface, which all ripened at the same time and had a good dose of pectins to give them consistency. The plant had to weigh half as much as the average plant. She crossed appropriate varieties and selected the Red Top variety, with its satisfactory architecture, to cross with the Tiny Tom, with fruits the size of a cherry.

The cultivation of the new tomato and its mechanical harvesting require more irrigation (because they are superficial plants), perfect fields, meticulous weed "control" so they don't obstruct the machines, and a course in the use

Growth hormone, which is given to livestock despite being carcinogenic for humans, earned almost three million dollars in 1998 for its discoverers and promoters: the University of Iowa. And the sales by distributors reached seventy million. Something similar occurred with the use of antibiotics as pesticides, prohibited in Europe because of the danger of resistant pathogenic microbes, but which continues to be used in the United States because of business interests.

and maintenance of the machines. But all this inconvenience is small when it comes to saving an industry. So, for the last fifteen years we have had excellent reddened tomatoes: small and dense, and probably sprayed with varnish to improve their outer appearance, since cosmetic research is common for fruits, including apples, peaches, citrus, and tomatoes. Chickens are also given xanthophylls so that their skin has a "pleasant yellow tint."

They have done and are conducting studies on consumer behavior and their preconceived ideas about the appearance of foods. The idea is to make people think that the food is "good." In this way, the University of Kansas Extension, by confirming that apples sell by the criteria of outer appearance more than nutrition, urges growers to produce a more attractive product, and that they beautify the displays in stores with mirrors and lights. The University of Iowa has studied the wrappers of foods, and it found that the color of ham was better conserved by vacuum packing or CO_2, thus attracting more consumers.

Alvaro Altés, biologist

Agrarian systems

Agrarian systems and eco-friendly alternatives

Intensive agriculture has only one goal—economic gain—and disregards the health of the planet entirely

Agriculture for life

Where do we want to end up? And where do we come from? Agriculture began ten thousand years ago in the Middle East, to the north of the Euphrates River or in the desert kites (see textbox). From there, it extended across the globe, although keep in mind that other areas have their own history. At the beginning, agriculture was extensive: they would plant one area until the yield diminished and then moved on to a new place, because there was enough space. It is similar to the slash-and-burn method still practiced in jungle regions today. To this type of agriculture, they added organic fertilizers that allowed the land to be used for many years. The fields were small, since they were tended by hand and required a lot of manual labor. The yields were reduced but enough to maintain a modest population.

The growth of the population and the needs of businesses gave rise to industrial agriculture, which uses large tracts of land to plant a single crop and fertilizes the land with chemical products to obtain maximum yields. It also introduces pesticides and herbicides to prevent the growth of weeds and insecticides to prevent insects from attacking the crops; it selects varieties with the highest yield per hectare, and uses machines to plant and harvest. The process suffers an adaptation period, since the first industrial crops were harvested by cheap manual labor: the combines in Europe and slaves in America.

Genetic engineering introduces species that are more resistant to drought, cold, heat, wet, altitude, and attacks by certain funguses or insects. These crops need chemical accessories that are only sold by the same company that makes the seed.

The desert kites

Many years ago, humans built traps out of stone in the shape of huge kites in the deserts of Syria and Jordan. Gazelles were trapped in large numbers during their migratory period, and they were slaughtered and conserved in salt, allowing the people to be at leisure the rest of the year. In this region, wild wheat and barley grew, and sheep grazed, not yet domesticated. It's not hard to believe that in this region under these circumstances, agriculture and livestock raising began and changed the life of humankind.

Modern agriculture is pushing out natural systems and causing the progressive poisoning of nature.

Monocropping, which consists of sowing a single species to make it most profitable, is associated with intensive agriculture. In some countries, monocropping coincides with the national needs, as happens in Thailand.

But, they have a high yield per hectare and are easy to harvest, store, conserve, and ripen.

Monocropping, which consists of sowing a single species to make it most profitable, is associated with intensive agriculture. In some countries, monocropping coincides with the national needs, as happens in Thailand with rice, but in others, the interests are those of a minority, such as in Ghana or Guinea with cacao (although, due to the high need for manual labor, a large part of the population benefits minimally).

In the face of this agriculture of profits, we find traditional agriculture practiced on a small scale, which applies modern knowledge to traditional methods, but without additives, herbicides, and insecticides that could be harmful to our health, based on the goal of obtaining a quality product that is, above all, healthier.

Industrial crops

In the case of some African countries in which there are food shortages, such as Ethiopia, they opt to dedicate great expanses of land to industrial crops and exports, such as sugar, cotton, or cacao. This deprives the people not only of the land they need to survive, but also the benefits of this type of agriculture. These are the most scandalous cases in modern agriculture.

The case of Japan

Japan is a super-populated country that needs to import the majority of its foods. It is small and mountainous, and only 14 percent of the land is suitable for agriculture. Thanks to its wet climate, half of its crops are flood crops and almost exclusively rice, a staple in all of southeast Asia. The rest are small plantations of soy, grains for humans (not animals), and fruit trees.

The average parcel is a hectare, but the majority are small parcels that the inhabitants use to plant vegetables part of the time. During the dry season, many rice paddies become rich vegetable gardens. In one such garden, Masanobu Fukuoka made his discoveries. This system of agriculture, based on quality products for direct consumption, is not very important to the Japanese economy.

The case of Guatemala

In the Cuchumatanes mountains, in the town of Todos Santos, not so long ago they grew corn, helped by an excellent climate and fertile lands. Between the corn stalks, they grew beans and squash. The harvest was abundant, although since the parcels were small, it was basically subsistence. They complemented this by trading corn for potatoes or coffee from the valley.

All this changed recently, when industrial agriculture appeared with the introduction of broccoli for exportation; farmers took out loans to buy seeds, irrigation systems, and pesticides. In exchange, they earned money to buy what they previously got from trading, and also clothing, radios, and televisions. The system put the population into debt, created unhappiness, and ended in failure.

Conventional agriculture

Conventional agriculture is essentially a polluter and a homogenizer, since it values quantity over quality and does not think twice about eliminating plagues or epidemics, unless there is a social outcry.

Conventional agriculture is also known as intensive agriculture. Its objective is to increase production at a lower cost. Until recently, the methods used were mainly genetic selection and hybridization through crossing different varieties to obtain more productive and resistant seeds.

In this type of agriculture, the use of herbicides and pesticides is the norm. The poisons used are increasingly more powerful and poisonous for the environment because plagues become resistant and need to be fought each year with more aggressive substances. There are specific ones that target a certain insect, or there are generic ones that, in order to kill a harmful fly, also kill off butterflies and dragonflies.

Recently and with the presumption of reducing the use of pesticides, genetic engineering has developed genetically modified products, which create plants resistant to diseases and plagues, but which carry other risks, such as the dependence of the grower on the company that produces the

seeds. They are required to sign exclusivity contracts so that, in addition to the seeds, they get all the related products they need from the same company.

The great dilemma is: at what point do the advantages outweigh the disadvantages? On a large scale, the development of industrial agriculture produces ever increasing yields, and in improbable places. On the contrary, defenders of biological agriculture maintain that you can produce the same amount through natural means, without contaminating the atmosphere or soil. A basic list of the main problems caused by conventional agriculture is:

Requires continual fertilization of the fields, which ends up polluting the soil and groundwater, especially with nitrates, which could come from inorganic fertilizers or the compounds produced on farms. There are already entire regions where it is inadvisable to drink the well water because of this.

The use of herbicides and pesticides that are stronger every year to eliminate weeds, poisons the environment and kills off numerous wild plants, useful insects, and even the birds and mammals that feed on them.

In addition to breaking the ecological balance, the use of pesticides causes, through natural selection, the survival of the most resistant weeds and harmful insects.

Genetically modified organisms

Theoretically, the businesses that produce seeds and chemical products for the fields are seeking alternatives that allow them to pollute less and increase production, without forgetting about the dependence of the growers on the crops. The result: genetically modified organisms, which are by definition living organisms artificially created by the introduction of genes of another being (virus, bacteria, plant, animal, or human). The result of this cross undoubtedly produces improved seeds, which, in addition to resisting plagues

Traditional corn, like that found in any province of Mexico or Guatemala, was cultivated by the indigenous people. Today, they are trying to save these varieties, which are better adapted to the environment, more resistant and, above all, self-sufficient. The seeds gathered each year by the farmers are enough to sow the following year, something impossible to do with genetically modified corn. (photo by Tiara)

and inclement weather, can grow in extreme conditions, which guarantees harvests and optimizes yields.

What are the inconveniences? In the first place, the dependence on the company that produces the seeds and the pesticides and herbicides, which are specific for the product and are applied on a smaller scale. As a result, we see the same effects on the environment that we saw before, to which we can add the issue of genetic erosion. But even more important, in the mid- and long-term, is the harm it can cause people: we're talking about allergies, antibiotic resistance, and the appearance of tumors from the accumulation of toxins.

In any case, genetic modification is a Pandora's box that, once opened, could bring about major alterations to the environment.

According to a report by the European Environmental Agency, there is no sure way to completely isolate genetically modified crops from others.

The isolation zones established—a distance of six meters between the crops and nearby vegetation, or barriers of different species—can't prevent extreme atmospheric conditions from dispersing the pollen long distances.

In Mexico, genetically modified contamination of corn has been confirmed to be the result of North American imports. In 2006, Greenpeace presented a document in Barcelona that demonstrated the impossibility of coexistence of genetically modified and traditional crops. It showed that the local contamination had already covered Aragon and Catalunya.

In 2005, in Australia, a group of genetically modified peas were developed, and fortunately not commercialized, that produced major changes in the immune systems of lab rats, causing them to develop allergies to the peas and other substances.

Genetically modified products

● **The varieties resistant to herbicides**, which allow the use of stronger poisons that destroy the environment and harm people.

● **Insecticidal plants**, agricultural crops modified to resist insects. The majority come from the bacteria, *Bacillus thuringiensis*, which is found in the soil. This bacteria causes disease in the harmful insects that ingest it, via a protein that is toxic to them. The genes of the bacteria responsible for producing the toxin are transferred to the plant and thus, a genetically modified plant is created.

● Genetically modified species also have the nickname of **terminator** because they are sterile and must always be bought from the same company.

Cross pollination

In the United States they tested a genetically modified grass for the greens of a golf course that was resistant to herbicides. In this way, they could eliminate all the weeds except that grass that was supposed to carpet around the hole. Afterward, it was demonstrated that cross pollination was very high within a radius of two kilometers of the grass, but its effects were even found in a sample more than twenty kilometers away.

Genetic erosion

In the year 2002, genetically modified organisms already made up 16 percent of the crops worldwide, in this order: soy, corn, and cotton, followed by wheat and sunflowers. The United States cultivates more than 80 percent and it invades the rest of the world from there. There's no way to be rid of them; flours made from GMO products are used in the production of 80 percent of prepared foods, from baby foods to cookies, and, above all, in the feeds given to the livestock that give us milk, meat, and eggs.

The list of those to blame is getting long. These companies have names: Monsato, Novartis, Aventis, DuPont, Bayer, Hi-Breed, and Astra-Zeneca. Monsato has been fined for their activity in many countries, and one type of genetically modified corn is prohibited in the United States.

The garden

They now produce genetically modified tomatoes, potatoes, and carrots, and probably peaches, lettuce, cucumbers, and apples. We can defend ourselves from products bought in the store, by choosing to plant our own gardens. If we want to be certain that our seeds won't be affected, we must confirm that there are no genetically modified crops in a radius of several kilometers. Otherwise, cross pollination is a risk for our garden, as are the pesticides and plagues that have genetically mutated to resist traditional methods of control. Some insects and bacteria have mutated once their natural enemies were killed off and have become dangerous, even for humans.

According to the FDA website, "Food and food ingredients derived from GE plants must adhere to the same safety requirements under the Federal Food, Drug, and Cosmetic (FD&C) Act that apply to food and food ingredients derived from traditionally bred plants.

"FDA encourages developers of GE plants to consult with the agency before marketing their products. Although the consultation is voluntary, [the director of the FDA's Office of Food Additive Safety, Dennis] Keefe says developers find it helpful in determining the steps necessary to ensure that food products made from their plants are safe and otherwise lawful.

"The developer produces a safety assessment, which includes the identification of distinguishing attributes of new genetic traits, whether any new material in food made from the GE plant could be toxic or allergenic when eaten, and a comparison of the levels of nutrients in the GE plant to traditionally bred plants."

"FDA scientists evaluate the safety assessment and also review relevant data and information that are publicly available in published scientific literature and the agency's own records.

"As of May 2013, FDA has completed 96 consultations on genetically engineered crops. A complete list of all completed consultations and our responses are available at www.fda.gov/bioconinventorywww.fda.gov/bioconinventory."

Because of this, it is important to have seed banks, to save your own seeds and to get new ones from other organic gardeners. Experience shows us that the yield can be even greater by practicing biologic agriculture, and, of course, the produce obtained is much more flavorful and healthy for the earth and you.

Subsidies

One problem associated with conventional agriculture is related to subsidies. Producing a ton of wheat does not cost the same in a wealthy country as it does in a poor country. Farmers need to earn a lot more money in the first world, and if the market worked freely, industries would buy from poor countries where the price is much lower. Subsidies (and the conventional agrarian methods that value quantity over

Genetically modified crops that have the highest risk of cross-pollination are the three most common: rapeseed, corn, and beets. The risk is lower in the case of barley, potatoes, and wheat.

GMOs and the problem of hunger

And how to solve the problem of hunger . . . Although they want to convince us otherwise, the problem of world hunger is not a matter of scarcity of food, but rather a matter of distribution, and access to land and seeds. A simple increase in production, promised by the biotech revolution (a mirage very far off, as the reality of developed GMO crops demonstrates) does not feed the most needy populations, but does dispossess them of their lands, their seeds, and more.

The prohibitive costs of new biotechnologies and the patents make them inaccessible to public research programs, favoring a worrisome amount of control over the sector by a handful of multinational agrochemical companies, whose only pursuit is to control the world markets and increase their profits.

The high price of patented seeds and the herbicides that go with them, and the characteristics of new varieties that are advantageous for large, fully mechanized operations, increases the marginalization of small local farmers. This will not solve the problem of hunger, but rather will endanger the means of subsistence for about half the world's population, which still lives off of agriculture. It also puts global biodiversity at risk and aggravates the problem of access to food for the poorest. Far from contributing to solving the problems of hunger, therefore, genetically modified crops and the monopoly on seeds via patents are a threat to sustainable agriculture, our health, and food security for many populations.

Ecologists in Action

quality) make it so that corn produced in the United States ends up being cheaper on the international market than that produced in Mexico, for example. This policy is bankrupting many Mexican farmers and blocks the development of agriculture in poorer countries. On the other hand, doing away with subsidies would abandon many growers in Europe and North America, which are major exporters of foods, and could produce problems in poor regions that are net importers, such as India. Governmental intervention that regulates the price of basic products, and the corporations that determine the price of industrial products such as cacao and coffee, have made agriculture an abused sector of the economy, from which only the owners benefit.

An alternative

The disappearance of subsidies would leave growers with only one alternative: the production of quality, organic products. Consumers are increasingly more health-conscious and aware of the dangers of manipulated foods. Industrial agriculture has no qualms about the use of herbicides and pesticides. What's more, it sets up shop in countries where the legislation gives more freedom in this regard. The future of agriculture must move toward recovering species that were cast aside for their lower productivity or incompatibility with machinery. The agriculture of the future must focus on quality and diversity. In this book, we will show that these qualities are not mutually exclusive with quantity and profits, as European wine and cheese produces have demonstrated.

An ecological prince

The Prince of Wales—who has distinguished himself for attacking English architects, in defense of an aesthetic in harmony with reason—published an article in the *Daily Telegraph* (1998) titled "The Seeds of Disaster." This positioned him alongside defenders of eco-friendly agriculture and, obviously, on our side. Unfortunately, the tabloid press in his country did not allow him to get more deeply involved in this cause, but his words remain. Below is an excerpt:

"I have always believed that agriculture should proceed in harmony with nature, recognising that there are natural limits to our ambitions. That is why, some 12 years ago, I decided to farm organically—without artificial pesticides or fertilisers. From my own experience I am clear that the organic system can be economically viable, that it provides a wide range of environmental and social benefits, and, most importantly, that it enables consumers to make a choice about the food they eat.

"(...) The fundamental difference between traditional and genetically modified plant breeding is that, in the latter, genetic material from one species of plant, bacteria, virus, animal or fish is literally inserted into another species, with which they could never naturally breed. The use of these techniques raises, it seems to me, crucial ethical and practical considerations.

I happen to believe that this kind of genetic modification takes mankind into realms that belong to God, and to God alone. Apart from certain highly beneficial and specific medical applications, do we have the right to experiment with, and commercialise, the building blocks of life? We live in an age of rights—it seems to me that it is time our Creator had some rights too.

"(...) We are told that GM crops will require less use of agro-chemicals. Even if this is true, it is certainly not the whole story. What it fails to take into account is the total ecological and social impact of the farming system. For example, most of the GM plants marketed so far contain genes from bacteria which make them resistant to a broad spectrum weedkiller available from the same manufacturer. When the crop is sprayed with this weedkiller, every other plant in the field is killed. The result is an essentially sterile field, providing neither food nor habitat for wildlife. These GM crop plants are capable of interbreeding with their wild relatives, creating new weeds with built-in resistance to the weedkiller, and of contaminating other crops. Modified genes from a crop of GM rape were found to have spread into a conventional crop more than a mile away. The result is that both conventional and organic crops are under threat, and the threat is one-way.

"(...) Once genetic material has been released into the environment it cannot be recalled. The likelihood of a major problem may, as some people suggest, be slight, but if something does go badly wrong we will be faced with the problem of clearing up a kind of pollution which is self-perpetuating. I am not convinced that anyone has the first idea of how this could be done, or indeed who would have to pay."

Prince of Wales

In the year 2004, the Chinese government approved the importation of genetically modified soy, cotton, and corn, adding themselves to the list of countries who have come to depend directly on American corporations.

Biodynamic agriculture

Rudolf Steiner (1861-1925) is the founder of biodynamic agriculture.

Biodynamic agriculture follows the principles set forth by **Rudolf Steiner,** the father of anthroposophy, in 1924, during a course given in Koberwitz. According to his teachings, there is an interrelation between matter and the cosmic forces of the universe.

Biodynamic agriculture, therefore, comes from the cooperation between the earth and mankind, maintaining a balance between the principles of matter and the immaterial world present in nature. All the processes of the fields—the preparation of the soil, the sowing, the rotation of crops, the harvest—should bear in mind the cosmic forces, that is to say, the stars, sun, moon, and planets, and the terrestrial forces, water, and mineral elements.

In order to make the soil and plants more receptive to these forces, one must use some special biodynamic preparations.

These preparations are made by a special composting technique, which puts new energy into organic compounds, to then mix them with the soil.

The principles of biodynamic agriculture

You must start with balanced soil, that is to say, it must be analyzed and its nutritive deficiencies corrected, for example, trace elements and an excess or lack of acidity.

The compost and biofertilizers used are simply vehicles for the biodynamic substances, herbs or homeopathic preparations of micronutrients that accelerate the decomposition of compost, will benefit the good microorganisms, and accelerate the growth of the plants.

The soil should be considered a living organism that has its own structure. You should avoid subsoiling too deeply, which breaks this structure, and use direct sowing. But leaving a poor-quality soil to its own devices does not help much either, so it should be prepared appropriately, as the previous points indicated. Also add in the presence of beneficial species, like some types of trees.

The grower should diversify the species to the maximum, in the forest, in the garden, or in the fields. The creation of new ecosystems always favors the proliferation of life and a greater quantity of biomass that gets recycled in the soil. You should favor rotation or succession of ecosystems, and experimentation.

Another important factor is the planning of the garden or fields: the paths, the tool shed, the silo, the fruit trees—basically, the distribution of elements.

Don't discard economic viability. At the end of the day, you want to benefit, whether in the form of food, or, in the case of a farm, a sufficient yield to sustain the experience.

And there is a spiritual aspect to biodynamic farming that must not be forgotten. The land should be considered a part of ourselves, that is, a part of the universe that we understand, although others prefer to consider it the body of Christ, and therefore, as something sacred. Its products are also sacred and should

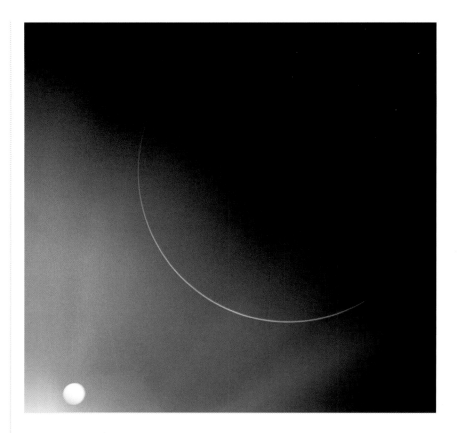

Extract of horsetail

This consists of boiling 50 grams in three liters of water for an hour. Strain and dilute in 20 liters. With this liquid, water the earth several times a year, especially in spring and fall. The water of horsetail harmonizes the earth and combats certain diseases, like mold and mildew.

be seen in this way. It is a way of giving importance to that which we make and to lend it part of our spiritual energy.

In order for all this to produce results, you should keep in mind the dynamic of the Cosmos, which is reflected in the biodynamic calendar—which is different every year, as it depends on the position of the stars. The stars indicate when to perform different tasks.

The most well-known calendar for planting is that of Maria Thun, a German farmer who has followed the principles of biodynamic farming for over fifty years. Maria confirmed that crops develop differently depending on the day they were planted, according to the position of the celestial bodies.

Finally, there are the biodynamic preparations, mediators between the earth and the Cosmos, which are vegetable, animal, and mineral extracts, usually fermented, dynamized by shaking, and then diluted before application.

Biodynamic preparations

There can be two kinds: preparations of medicinal herbs introduced by Steiner, which harmonize the soil-plant-cosmos relationship, and preparations from compost, extracts of humic acids that prepare the plant to take advantage of cosmic influences. Although the dosage is not calculated mathematically, they can be bought commercially and there are a series of methods that must be done with certain precision. The plants used in these preparations are as common as chamomile, fennel, dill, nettle, or horsetail.

Basic preparations

The basic preparations are divided into two kinds: those that are sprayed on the ground and plants, and those that inoculate the compost or other organic marinades as biofertilizers.

The preparations are numbered from 500 to 508. The first two, 500 and 501, are preparations of manure and silica. Preparation 500 of silica is made by burying the horn of a cow filled with manure, medicinal plants, and even pulverized quartz, for the entire summer. Then it is dug up, diluted with a large quantity of water, and distributed over the earth in a fine mist, providing it with a large quantity of microorganisms. In this way, there is no need to fight plagues because we give the earth the means to fight them itself.

The use of biodynamic preparations can cause an increase in infestations and diseases for the first year, but it has been shown to reduce these with continued use.

Preparations for the compost

These are made from six plants: yarrow, chamomile, nettle, oak, dandelion, and valerian. These represent the digestive processes of nature, so for their production they are placed in the peritoneum, intestine, or bladder of an animal, where they are left to age for at least a winter.

The Moon

After Rudolf Steiner described the influences of the stars on the lives of plants, others began to investigate the influence of the moon.

The result is that in order to have a good harvest, you should keep in mind the position of the moon with respect to the zodiac constellations, before which it remains for two days.

- **Leafy plants** should be planted during a water zodiac sign: Cancer, Scorpio, or Pisces.

- **Seed plants and fruits** should be planted in a fire sign: Aries, Leo, or Sagittarius.

- **Root plants** require an earth constellation: Taurus, Virgo, or Capricorn.

- **And flowers should be planted** with an air constellation: Gemini, Libra, or Aquarius.

In any case, you must also keep in mind the phases of the moon. If it is waxing and the energy is in full swing, it is a good time to graft and plant rapidly germinating plants, but you shouldn't prune the trees. **If the moon is waning**, it is a good time to prune and work the soil deeply.

The theory is that the manure has captured the astral forces upon passing through the intestine of the animal, and the buried horn preserves these forces and strengthens them. There could be a lot of biology in all this, since the horn when buried at certain depths causes an increase in microbial activity where previously there was none. This preparation is also called the "Preparation of Light," since it attracts the effects of the sun, favoring the root system.

The next six preparations, yarrow (502), chamomile (503), nettle (504), oak (505), dandelion (506), and valerian (507) serve as complements to compost, manure, or biofertilizer.

To make the preparation from chamomile (503), the flowers are picked and dried in the summer, dampened with chamomile extract, and placed in the small intestine of a cow, where they are left all winter to be used in the spring.

The preparation from oak (505) consists of putting the bark of the tree in the skull of a cow or sheep, putting it in a hole or a barrel, and letting it soak with rain water. The preparation of yarrow (502) requires putting the flowers of this plant in the urinary bladder of a deer.

Dynamization

This is the final phase. When a biodynamic preparation is diluted in water, it should be stirred rhythmically in a circular motion, which will transfer the powers of the preparation into the water. The water is stirred by hand or by a special machine, in one direction. This will create a vortex or whirlpool in the mixture, representative of a determined order. Suddenly, this order should be reversed, stirring in the opposite direction. The chaos created will transmit the forces from the preparation to the water. There are other conditions, such as that the water must be 37 degrees Celsius. You should use a container made of natural materials and not stainless steel. The vortex should reach 85 percent of the maximum height of the container, and the rotation should last an

In Europe, it is common to add a mixture of basalt dust and crushed eggshells to the manure used in the preparations.

hour, without timing it. It should never be done with more than 250 liters of water, so the water entraps the life.

Animal infestations

Biodynamic agriculture has diverse options for combating plagues and infestations. If they are from insects or snails, begin by burning some in a wood fire during the appropriate constellation. The ash that is left should be ground for an hour in a mortar and pestle. Of this ash, dilute one gram in nine grams of water and shake for three minutes, obtaining a D1 dilution. This action should be performed eight times, until you reach a D8 dilution. Then, this liquid should be sprayed over the crops three afternoons in a row, to end the infestation.

The plants and the cosmos

Influence of the celestial bodies on the growth of plants

BODY	FAVORS
Sun	Orange, saffron, sunflower, cinnamon, chamomile, dandelion, rosemary, marigold, olive, passionflower, and mistletoe.
Moon	Irises, willow, honeysuckle, watercress, chard, melons, and cucumbers.
Mercury	Anise, parsley, fennel, and lavender.
Mars	Thistle, roses, blackberries, raspberries, peppers, carrots, garlic, mustard, basil, hawthorn, aloe, nettle, arnica, tobacco, and geraniums.
Venus	Irises, apples, poppies, orchids, violets, elder, lemongrass, thyme, birch, yarrow, alder tree, and primrose.
Jupiter	Cabbage, cauliflower, grapes, figs, olives, blackberries, acorns, nuts, oregano, jasmine, and lemon balm.
Saturn	Horsetail, hemlock, deadly nightshade, holly, plantain, valerian, onion, mosses, potatoes, and eggplant.

Alfredo Luis Pepi (buenasiembra.com.ar)

Permaculture

Permaculture is the design of sustainable human habitats, following Nature's guide.

It was developed in 1970 by two Australian ecologists, Bill Mollison and David Holmgren, to offer an alternative to industrial agriculture and the destruction of nature, which was occurring in their country at a shocking rate. The three basic principles of permaculture are:

Integrate care for the land, the care of people, and the exact yield in an ethical manner. That is, grow only what is necessary, in a way that is appropriate for you, keeping in mind the needs of the land.

Use the ecologic principles derived from the observation of natural systems.

The use of tools and processes in a way that requires the minimum use of resources for its implementation and maintenance.

Ethical principles

The ethics of caring for the earth is possibly the most difficult principle to understand. Therefore, many have sought a way to explain it. One of the simplest can be found at the Permaculture Association of Aldehuela, in Spain. Summarized, its main points are the following:

Care for the earth, keeping in mind sustainability, fertility, and the use of natural energy such as the sun; planning on the small scale and recycling.

Care for people, stimulating mutual help between individuals and communities

Redefine necessities and sow a possible future, according to the equation: Population x lifestyle = required load capacity.

Principles of design

Permaculture focuses a lot on the harmony of the garden with Nature. For these purposes, it upholds the following principles:

Work in favor of nature, not against it.

Everything is part of the garden, including the slugs, which can help us clean up the lettuce patch.

The limits of the harvest are in your imagination, since everything can help increase its yield. What's more, that which is or isn't beneficial is in your way of looking at things.

All that we use has its positive and negative side, its advantages and disadvantages, and the way you utilize it will determine your ability to obtain maximum yield.

You should carefully observe nature to make the minimum changes (or minimum intervention) in order to obtain maximum yield.

In addition to these elemental principles, the permaculturist should bear in mind that the garden contains diverse microclimates, since the presence of a tree or a slope have a notable influence on the plants. You must also remember the limits of the garden; protect against plagues and external factors in many ways at once; consider the relationship between the plants and arrange them so that they benefit from each other; value diversity; and, above all, think on the small scale, even if the garden is large.

A way to achieve ecological sustainability of the planet

Permaculture is a system of design for the creation of sustainable human environments. The objective is to create systems that are ecologically sustainable and economically viable, that satisfy needs, that don't exploit or pollute, and that are self-sufficient in the long term. Permaculture deals with plants, animals, construction, and infrastructure (water, energy, communications), not just as elements in and of themselves, but in relation to each other. The basis is the observation of natural ecosystems, along with the ancestral wisdom of primitive peoples and scientific knowledge. It tries to use the inherent qualities of the plants and animals combined with the natural characteristics of the land and structures in order to produce a system that supports life in the city or country, using as little space as possible. It tries to work with Nature and not against it.

Permacultura-es.org: Bill Mollison,
Introduction to Permaculture

The basic principle of permaculture is to "work for" or "in favor of," not "against," nature.

Since 1980, permaculture has spread across the globe, thanks to a group of volunteer students who learned from its creators. A country like Zimbabwe has more than fifty specialized schools on the science.

Bioenergetic plots

The Earth is crossed continuously by a series of subtle energies that have a notable effect on living beings. The main one is an electromagnetic field, which converts the planet into a gigantic magnet crisscrossed by magnetic lines between the North and South poles, and which, among other things, can contribute to the orientation of migratory birds.

There are other natural forces, which have to do with the rocky substratum, geologic faults, or currents of subterranean water. The energy given off by one of these phenomena can be more or less intense, and can be positive or negative. In ancient times, geomancers determined if a place was favorable to construct a house or not, and even today it is practiced in places like Germany. Remember that nomadic groups like the gypsies only camped in places that the dogs chose to lie down to rest, since these animals always avoid places with negative energy.

Hartmann lines

Among the natural energies that influence the growth of plants are those called Hartmann lines, discovered by the German doctor of the same name and by Manfred Curry. These are an invisible energy that covers the whole planet in the form of a screen. Doctor Peyre, who formed the hypothesis of its existence, defined it thusly:

"This deals with a north-south radiation, apparently magnetic and caused by the magnetism of the earth, and an east-west radiation, perpendicular to the other and of an electric appearance. They are rectilinear radiations, so they cannot be a result of different terrestrial influences, like the composition of the soil or the presence of faults in the subsoil or subterranean water flow, which are always winding and cut through the earth's crust along a variable path, accidents of the soil. They cover our sphere in a net that demarcates

The **Hartmann net** is like a net of square mesh, most evident from a bird's eye view of the crops.

Hartmann lines and trees

Isidoro Zudaire, an ecological grower in Guadalajara, has proved that:

Firs, acacias, chestnuts, holm oaks, rubber plants, ash, oaks, and elder trees **resist** negative zones.

Hazelnuts, fig trees, plum trees, black poplars, mulberries, and grape vines **tolerate** them.

Cherries, peach trees, walnuts, elms, pear trees, bananas, lime trees, and arborvitae **do not resist** negative zones.

square neutral zones, compartmentalizing the soil and extending into the air, crossing over in the north-south and east-west direction . . ."

Peyre even demonstrated that there was a certain relationship between these lines or bands, which cover the entire planet, and cancer. But the one who truly developed the theory was doctor Hartmann: "The earth is covered with a global network of fixed waves that seem to be produced by terrestrial radiation coming from the interior of the planet which are ordered in a mesh-like shape when going through the layers of the earth's crust."

The dangerous spots are those where the energetic lines cross. The bands of energy go up as high as two thousand meters, are about 25 centimeters thick, and are arranged parallel every two and a half meters when oriented north to south, and every two meters east to west. These bands can be wider in the case of disturbances such as earthquakes, and undulate following the terrain. The intersections of these lines are harmful to humans, the lines alone less so, and the spaces in the squares are harmless.

Animals have a special sensitivity to detect these places. For example, dogs will flee from them, while cows, hens, and horses suffer illnesses if they are forced to stay in these places, and even bees produce less honey if the hive is placed where it shouldn't be. Only cats, among domesticated animals (and ants, among other animals) are able to benefit from these energies, which indicates that you shouldn't choose a cat's resting spot for yourself or your plants, since the energies don't harm the cats.

Energetic networks and the garden

You must keep in mind that we are talking about a complementary system, which adds control over a series of energies to the necessary organic practices in order to obtain a better yield from our garden. The energies to keep in mind are: the cosmic energies (of

the stars) and earthly energies, among which are the Hartmann net, and those caused by faults, caves, gases, or underground water currents. These energies influence the plants and animals that act on them.

Furrows

Our relationship with the energetic lines starts and ends in the design of the garden, and in this respect, the arrangement of the plants, that is to say, the furrows. These should be dug from north to south, between the Hartmann lines, which are wider in this direction, and you should make two or three furrows in the two and a half meters between the lines. It is best to measure them with a pendulum to be certain of the width. The Hartmann lines from east to west don't have as much influence on plants, but Isidoro Zudaire of Salamanca, Spain recommends you plant cover crops like clover, alfalfa, or legumes in rotation with grains in the areas where the lines cross. These crops, once cut, will serve to cover and fertilize the furrows with organic material. The negative zones of the Hartmann lines are favorable for the growth of weeds, fungus, and bacteria, mineral deficiencies, and plagues.

The Fukuoka Method

We must sow and sow if we want to offer a future to our descendants.

Masanobu Fukuoka

Fukuoka inspiration

Inspiration came to Fukuoka one day when, passing through the countryside, he discovered some rice plants flourishing in an abandoned field. He decided that he had to sow his plants when the seeds naturally fell to the ground, in autumn, rather than spring, as tradition dictates. He would avoid weeds with a cover crop of clover and he would interfere as little as possible with the natural process of the soil.

The method

This method, widespread in Japan, manages to obtain two harvests, one of rice in the summer and one of grains, wheat or barley, in the winter. The extraordinary part of this is that it does not require fertilizer or preparation of the land, but rather that the land be respected as is and enriched each year. The yield is equal to that of chemical agriculture and the system has a natural philosophical compo-nent that adapts perfectly to the climate fluctuations of the area. The rainy season, dominated by monsoons, allows for the cultivation of rice in a short period of time. The rest of the year, with generous rain, Fukuoka uses a series of tricks which he has taught all across the country and has developed for many years. For example, the substrata of the base is formed by a layer of clover that protects the land from erosion and gives natural fertilizer, since it is a good assimilator of nitrogen. The clover dies off during the flooding, allow-ing for the sowing of rice, but it re-sprouts every year.

The seeds of the rice, barley, and wheat are mixed with clay and wet until they form little balls, which are placed on top of a layer of decomposing straw in the autumn. Then, you add another layer of grass and straw harvested the same year as the rice and grain. With the damp earth added, the seeds sprout and go through the straw underneath to reach the soil. The clover will sprout again when the grain is already tall enough to not be affected, and then the clover helps hold moisture. The rye and barley sprout quickly and are harvested in May, but the rice waits until spring. The wheat and barley straw is left to dry on the ground, then it is a collected, and, once the grain is separated, the straw is ground and laid out once more on the ground as a cushioning. The monsoon floods of June weaken the grass and then the rice grows.

The philosophy of doing nothing

This is the name given to Fukuoka's philosophy, whose fundamental principle involves the idea that purifying the spirit and healing the earth are the same process. One has to wonder what would happen if one did nothing. And the conclusion is that you should not plow the soil, you should not use chemical fertilizers or prepared composts, you shouldn't remove weeds with herbicides and, in general, you shouldn't use chemical products for no reason.

Fukuoka's five principles

1 **No working the land**

2 **No fertilizers**

3 **No pesticides**

4 **No weeding**

5 **No pruning**

In Japan, the spirit of permaculture has manifested in the extraordinary personality, Masanobu Fukuoka, through the publication of his book, *One Straw Revolution*. In the images, Fukuoka during a famous course in Ibiza.

Nendo dango

Nendo dango is the Japanese name for the balls of clay that Fukuoka has discovered to be the most efficient way to plant seeds. The seeds are covered in a layer of clay, the thickness of which depends on the size of the seed. This is left on the ground in the fall, well before germination.

The clay prevents the seeds from being eaten by birds or rodents, and when it rains, the clay absorbs moisture.

There are two ways to make these: manually, one by one, and mechanically, using a cement mixer with the blades removed. Fukuoka travels the world teaching his method to recover desert regions that should

not be considered deserts, such as the southeast of Spain, which he considers a rocky desert. In this case, one must select at least a hundred different seeds, including those of wild trees and fruit trees, grains, legumes, and vegetables in order to get a two percent germination—ten times higher than in conventional sowing—and recuperate the land.

Synergetic agriculture

The idea of **synthesizing** the most advanced methods of alternative agriculture is **thrilling.**

Emilia Hazelip

The four principles of synergy

1 Don't plow the land

2 Don't fertilize. The self-fertilizing of the land is enough.

3 Don't use chemical products.

4 Don't compress the soil.

This is a model of production so that the land fertilizes itself, based on the natural agriculture without the labor of Masanobu Fukuoka, created and developed by Emilia Hazelip around the year 1987. She synthesized the methods of Ruth Stout (cultivating without working the land), the plots of Alan Chatwick, the work of Fukuoka, and permaculture.

In Emilia's words: "Personally, I believe that having to deconstruct the soil and keep it fertile artificially, fattening it up with fertilizers, compost, etc. is a mistake that has been repeated since the beginning of agriculture, and it's time to correct this practice which is responsible for so much erosion of the planet."

Her system notably accelerates the start-up process of a garden; it takes barely ten days to start one, but one must follow her methods for at least three years to obtain the desired yield. Synergy is, by definition, "the action of two or more causes that produce one effect that is superior to the sum of the individual effects." It deals with maintaining coherence between all the elements that make up the garden: the soil, the plants and animals, and the interaction between them all will produce the desired result.

The garden

Make patches that are 48 inches wide and 20 inches high, with 32 inches between them. Cover them with a cushion that will serve as a protective filter between the surface of the soil and the atmosphere, which will protect from the drying of the sun and prevent compaction caused by rain. You can use straw or dry grass, but also wool or cardboard, or any other organic scrap that protects and favors the existence of beneficial living things, such as earthworms. The only area of soil that is left clean is a small margin around the crops. Except for root crops like potatoes and carrots, everything else should be left to rot in the soil, so that it contributes to creating a permanent humus layer on the soil. This is why it takes at least three years.

Patience is one of the necessary virtues for ecological gardening if you want to become self-sufficient.

Biointensive organic agriculture

Biointensive agriculture allows you to obtain a very high yield from a small parcel of land, since it takes advantage of all the layers of soil and light with plants that grow and take root to different heights.

This is a technique that has begun to be applied in third-world countries. The reason is in its definition: a system of food production on the small scale, centered on the unity of family production, with the use of available resources and an intensive use of manual labor over capital.

The method

First of all, it uses narrow, elevated beds which should not be walked on, and which are dug twice as deep as normal—that is, about 20 to 24 inches (which is known as *double bêchage* in French, or *double dug* in English).

Secondly, it uses compost abundantly and a large quantity of organic material. But it does not use inorganic fertilizers or those derived from petroleum, which have been proven to deteriorate the soil and pollute the earth.

Third of all, you must plant intensively, so that the soil is always protected from solar radiation by a layer of plants. This increases the yield. The leaves of the plants should touch, and they should all be at different heights. The microcli-mate created retains moisture, protects microscopic fauna of the soil, and the plants don't mature too quickly.

Fourth, it uses a combination of other species that benefit mutually from each other's company, like green beans and strawberries, for example. Always sow local plants and varieties that are resistant to plagues and disease.

It is necessary to rotate between types of plants: tubers, leafy greens, fruits, legumes, etc.

The system is an accelerated producer of organic material that will be used for compost.

The planting of tubers makes this system a high source of calories. To do so, 30 percent of the land should be occupied by potatoes, garlic, or parsnips.

This favors free pollination between all the plants; modified species are not necessary, genetic diversity is conserved, and the grower does not have to buy prepared seeds every year.

Finally, one should plant every type of plant in the garden each year, although in different places.

The Soil Association

In England there are many associations devoted to nature conservation. Some even buy land to conserve it as nature dictates. Their enthusiasm went as far as to buy alpine meadows in Switzerland after World War I so that their beauty was not disturbed, but they made the mistake of not allowing cows to graze there. Soon those rocky hillsides were taken over by new, emergent forests, since their green perfection had been maintained by those underrated ruminants.

But we learn from our mistakes, and since then many years have passed. The Soil Association was founded in 1946 to find an alternative to the industrialization of agricultural production. Its starting point was the soil erosion caused by modern methods. Because of this, the land loses nutrients and its health deteriorates.

The goal of the Soil Association is to combine the best of the old ways with the new, and return the land to its natural richness. Based on the experiences of Albert Howard with the Indians, and his disciple Eve Balfour, they developed a system that is based on two techniques: composting and soil rotation.

> A biointensive planting would be one that combines corn, green beans, and pumpkins. The beans climb the corn stalks, while the pumpkins sprawl across the ground between the corn rows, taking maximum advantage of the space.

Compost

Composting is the basis of the biologic farm, and its function is to recycle. It takes into account all the elements that form part of the soil: nutrients, worms, beetles, fungus, bacteria, microorganisms, minerals, water, and air.

Rotation

If we grow the same species in the same plot of land each year, the least abundant minerals will be used up and the health of the soil and plants will decline. For the Soil Association, rotation is the spirit of biologic agriculture. The important thing is to return to the soil that which we have taken from it the previous year, by growing different species.

Enemies of the soil

The main enemy of the soil is agrochemical products, that is, fertilizers and pesticides. These worsen the condition of the soil, are needed in higher quantities each year, and their effects are more harmful each time, causing a vicious cycle.

Inorganic fertilizers only give the soil nitrogen, phosphorus, and potassium, and their production consumes petroleum. They are easily washed into rivers and pollute the and adjacent lands, as we already know.

Genetically modified plants are developed to combat the degradation of the soil, caused by fertilizers and pesticides. Their effects on our health remain unknown, the environmental contamination caused by cross pollination with wild species is also unknown, and in any case, irreversible and uncontrollable. As if that weren't enough, these types of crops create dependency among farmers, which makes them poorer. All of these aspects are widely addressed in other parts of this book.

Vegetable-flower garden

The *acequia*, from the Arab word **al-saqiya** (irrigation channel), is the channel through which water is distributed from the reservoir to the garden. The precious liquid flows downhill to the furrows, where it is filtered and absorbed by the plants.

The expression defines itself: The garden should contemplate forms and be not just a source of healthy and natural foods, but also a way to satisfy our spirit and give the beauty that all of us need around us to feel good.

If you let yourself follow your tastes, you will probably obtain the desired effect, but a little help to achieve the proper balance would not hurt. Given that the majority of ornamental plants have an edible component, it should not be hard to find the combination of medicinal and aromatic herbs, vegetables, and fruits that will bring beauty to your vegetable-flower garden on the balcony, in the terrace, or in the country, using the space you have reserved for it. The parcel of land should not exceed ten or fifteen square meters per person it will feed.

The Muslim vegetable-flower garden

In the ancient Islamic Spain, the garden was more than a simple esthetic arrangement of plants. It contained aromatic plants, fruit trees, and horticultural products, all connected by an ingenious distribution of water.

There is a work in Arabic titled *The Book of Agriculture*, written in verse so it could be easily remembered, which contains basic instructions: the garden should be divided in plots separated by paths or aisles covered with vines. At its head, there will be a reservoir from which you water the garden. Next to it, in one of the plots, are the aromatic plants, then the flower beds and fruit trees, the vines and fig trees, and finally the biggest trees, such as cherries and plums, on the north face, to protect the garden from wind.

In the Arabic garden, three elements are singularly important: the waterwheel, the reservoir, and the irrigation channel.

The *nuria* (na'ura) (waterwheel)

Even in modern times, we shouldn't discount the use of a waterwheel if we find ourselves close to a water current. In this way, we could do without electricity. The waterwheel is a wheel whose base is situated in running water. The wheel is made up of buckets that fill with water when they pass the bottom and empty at the top, into channels that direct the water into a reservoir or irrigation channel. In places where the water does not have enough force to push the wheel, such as in ponds or wells, they used water wheels powered by animals, generally donkeys. This same system can be implemented with wind power.

The *alberca* (al-birka) (reservoir)

This is an important element of this vegetable-flower garden, since in addition to allowing for calm, measured watering, it also is an esthetic element. You can grow water lentils or keep fish, and it is a refreshing element of the garden, around which the cherries and fig trees grow, and the farmer can rest and eat in the shade.

The *acequia* (al-saqiya) (irrigation channel)

This is the basis of the irrigation system, the channels through which water is distributed from the reservoir, a dam, a waterwheel, or sometimes a pump. This name encompasses both the major channels, that can be observed on the banks of the Nile River to water the fields of grains, and the minor ones, which go through the fields and branch out. In a small family garden, it will be enough to have one channel that crosses the garden and a series of temporary ones, opened and closed with a hoe when necessary.

This process constitutes one of the most pleasurable moments of the work day, in which the water, the source of life, floods clean furrows and feeds your plants.

The Arabic orchard

The vision of a garden in medieval, Arabic Spain was very different from that which we have now. Without tomatoes and potatoes, they instead had date palms. These are still the staple of Egyptian gardens (there are over two hundred species), where it is easy to find dates of all colors drying in the sun in September. Other trees that decorate the garden were peach, lemon, orange, cherry, quince, and pomegranate trees. If the land was favorable, they grew a large fig tree, and if not, some trellises with vines.

On the ground, melons, watermelons, eggplants, beans, spinach, carrots, artichokes, lettuce, kidney beans, cabbages, chickpeas, peas, lentils, garlic, onions, and countless useful plants grew; everything except the American products that had not yet come to Europe, such as corn, potatoes, tomatoes, sunflowers, cacao, and tobacco grew. Some aromatic plants were found in the country and considered poor people's foods, such as oregano, thyme, and basil. As far as nuts, they ate almonds, hazelnuts, walnuts, and pine nuts that were harvested in the country. But they also grew olives, which produced oil, processed at home or at a local mill.

Arabic cooking

They say that you can live for three weeks on a single date, but perhaps **if we bring some sweet biscuits, made from honey, hazelnuts, almonds, cinnamon, anise, cloves** (brought by the Arabs in the Middle Ages from the Maluku Islands), cilantro, sesame, sugar, and flour, without modern eggs and milk, **we could survive much longer**. Arabic cooking, because of its long tradition, is incredibly rich and includes lemon preserves, pickled green olives, eggplant pâté, mint and cucumber soup, hummus, falafel, lentil soup, and many other things. And that's not even getting into the couscous.

Basic rule for organic agriculture from IFOAM

The base for plant production

Gardening, agriculture, or the forest systems should take into account the structure and fertility of the surrounding ecosystem, and with this knowledge, strive for maximum diversity of species and minimal loss of nutrients. To do so, utilize:

● **A rotation of versatile crops**, including legumes.

● **An appropriate ground cover during as much of the year as possible**, and with maximum diversity of plant species.

The IFOAM, International Federation of Organic Agriculture Movements, has published a small manual to establish conditions that organic agriculture must meet:

● Produce foods with high nutritive quality and in sufficient quantities.
● Interact constructively with the natural systems and cycles.
● Keep in mind the wide social and ecological impact of the organic production and processing systems.
● Promote and intensify the biologic cycles within the agrarian system, which involves an understanding of microorganisms, the flora and fauna of the soil, plants, and animals.
● Develop a valuable and sustainable aquatic ecosystem.
● Maintain and increase the fertility of the soil in the long term.
● Maintain genetic diversity in the productive system and its surroundings, including the protection of habitats for wild plants and animals.

● Promote the careful use and appropriate care of water, aquatic resources, and the life they sustain.
● Employ, as much as possible, renewable resources in locally organized agrarian systems.
● Create a harmonic balance between agricultural production and livestock.
● Provide livestock with living conditions that take into account their basic functions and innate behaviors.
● Minimize all forms of possible pollution.
● Process organic products using renewable resources.
● Produce ecological products that are completely biodegradable.
● Allow all those involved in the agricultural production and processing to lead a life that will cover their basic needs and allow them to obtain adequate income and satisfaction from their work, including a safe work environment. Progress toward a chain of production, processing, and distribution that is socially sustainable.

Fertilization

One must return sufficient quantities of biodegradable microbial, vegetable, or animal material to the soil, to improve or at least maintain the fertility and biologic activity.

The base of fertilization programs should be made up of biodegradable material of microbial, vegetable, or animal origin, produced on organic farms.

To do so, they recommend:

● The handling of fertilization should minimize the loss of nutrients.

● One should prevent the accumulation of heavy metals and other contaminants.

● Non-synthetic mineral fertilizers and biologic fertilizers brought to the farm should be considered supplements, and not a replacement for the recycling of nutrients.

● One should maintain adequate pH levels in the soil.

Disease control

Systems of organic agriculture should be managed in a way that minimizes losses caused by plagues, diseases, and weeds. You should prioritize the use of crops and varieties adapted to the environment, a balanced fertilization program, fertile soils with intense biologic activity, adequate rotation, association of crops, green manure, etc. The growth and development should occur naturally.

Weeds, plagues, and diseases should be controlled with different preventative cultural techniques that limit their development, for example, adequate rotation, green manure, a balanced fertilization program, early preparation of the land and pre-sowing, covering the soil (mulch), mechanical control, and interference in the life cycle of infestations. The natural enemies of plagues and diseases should be protected and encouraged, through appropriate management of the habitat to provide them places to live and nest.

Management of infestations must come from knowing and inferring the ecological necessities for them to flourish.

Genetic engineering

There is no place for genetic engineering in organic agriculture and processing. **Genetic engineering is a group of techniques of molecular biology** (such as recombinant DNA) through which the genetic material of plants, animals, microorganisms, cells, and other biologic units can be altered in ways or with results that could not be obtained through natural processes of reproduction or crossing.

Chilean nitrate and all synthetic nitrogenous fertilizers, including urea, are prohibited.

AGRARIAN SYSTEMS AND ECOLOGIC ALTERNATIVES

Conventional agriculture and GMO crops

Industrial crops and mono crops of rice, sugar, cotton, coffee, cacao, bananas, tea, vegetables, and grains, mainly to feed livestock, use more and more GMO seeds and chemical products. Fertilizers with excess nitrogen pollute water sources.

Integrated agriculture

Differentiated from conventional agriculture in that the use of chemical products is reduced by nearly half, and elements of organic agriculture are introduced. Requires a higher technical element, for example, soil analysis to add the necessary chemical fertilizers, without saturating the ground with harmful elements.

Permaculture

Developed by Bill Mollison and David Holmgren in Australia, it mainly supports the design and distribution of spaces around the house so that plants and animals help each other grow in harmony, for example, protecting the garden from north winds with a barrier of fruit trees, and these with bigger trees.

Bioenergetic plots

As the name indicates, this is biologic or organic because it does not use chemical products, and it is energetic due to the use of cosmic and terrestrial energies. The former come from the moon and stars, and the latter from the different forces that go through the earth and influence the growth and health of plants.

Biodynamic agriculture

Introduced in 1924 by Rudolf Steiner, the father of anthroposophy, in a famous conference in Koberwitz, this is the basis of the entire alternative movement and has given way to numerous branches. It was Albert Howard who put this into practice in India. It is based in composting, biodynamic preparations, and cosmic influences.

Ecologic agriculture

Rejects the use of chemical products and opts for maintaining the richness of the soil through crop rotation, avoiding erosion, and using biological systems to combat infestations. Developed in the five continents, there are different methods associated with different masters or cultures.

Biointensive agriculture

The objective is to make a self-sufficient garden using only organic methods and manual tools, with a high yield and a low consumption of energy. It was created by Alan Chatwick to combine the biodynamic and intensive horticulture systems, with high and soft beds. It is called the "edible landscape."

Natural agriculture according to the Fukuoka method

Developed by the Japanese master Masanobu Fukuoka, it emphasizes the respect for the land, sowing appropriate plants in the proper moment without plowing the land at all. Its starting point is in the question: Is doing this necessary? and his philosophy is summed up as the method of doing nothing.

Vegetable-flower garden

This is a garden in which the aesthetic aspect is important, so it combines vegetable plants with ornamental plants that are helpful in controlling plagues or attracting useful insects, and thus favor the growth of crops.

Get to know the soil

Nature and in-depth preparation of the soil

The best soils in the world are found in volcanic zones of the Caribbean, but if you put your mind to it, you can have better soil in your garden.

Soil covered in plants is protected from erosion. When you remove a layer of vegetation in order to plant or to eliminate a forest, the earth is easily washed away by rain. This would not happen if the soil was mixed with stubble of past crops, or if selective logging was used.

The composition and structure of the soil are important factors in the growth of plants. If you are trying to have a small balcony garden, the problem of composition decreases because you will buy conditioned soil, with all the elements that it needs to help plants grow well. But if you have a plot of land from which you want to obtain a good yield, it is best to know its characteristics before you begin working. The nature of the soil you are dealing with depends on the climate that has eroded and modified it, and the historic use of the area.

Fertility

The most fertile soils in the world are found in volcanic regions, and the most productive are those that also receive abundant rainfall; this is the case of the volcanic chain that traverses the western part of the America continent, the Ring of Fire that goes around the oceans and includes Japan, the Philippines, Hawaii, the Azores, and the Canary Islands.

If you are lucky enough to live in one of these places, or in Jamaica or Costa Rica, you can use the soil just as you find it.

The poorest soils are found in very rainy places formed from ancient soils, granite above all, which have been washed away for thousands of years by precipitation that took with it all the essential components. Large areas of the Amazon have very infertile soils that, once cleared of the vegetation that feeds it, becomes compact, rusty, and hard, and in turn absolutely unproductive because they are formed from just a single chemical compound.

In Venezuela, under the Roraima ridge, there are huge extensions of the sandy terrain that are only capable of producing grasslands, in a place where abundant rainfall and high annual temperatures should sustain tropical jungles. In Spain, the poorest regions are found in Galicia, where

The water cycle

 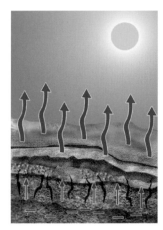  

The lack of vegetation makes it so that only part of the water soaks into the soil; the majority is lost in runoff, and, what's worse, takes away fertile soil with it, provoking soil erosion.

The ground heats up faster, and more intensely than vegetation. In places with bare soil, heat is greater and the evaporation of water more intense. The soil cracks and the capillarization makes the water disappear more quickly.

The function of trees is varied: not only do they protect the ground from the sun, but the fallen leaves give a humid layer that enriches it. On the other hand, wooded areas attract rain, retain water in the damp soil, and prevent erosion.

Evapotranspiration of the trees puts a large quantity of moisture into the air. Water goes up from the roots and evaporates from the leaves, while these perform their chlorophyllic function and trap CO_2 from the atmosphere.

---

the granitic soil is frequently washed by rain. This same type of soil in Extremadura, Spain, which has more moderate rainfall, is much richer. In the Iberian Peninsula, where the richest soils are found in the flat lands along rivers, erosion caused by deforestation and intensive use of the land for thousands of years has caused a major loss of fertile soil, as well as practically the entire moist layer.

Historic wear

The historic wear on the soil is an important factor, especially in Europe, where they have practiced agriculture for thousands of years. In America, the majority of the land has remained untouched until relatively recently, and are notably productive (except for natural disasters such as droughts, floods, or cold spells), but in Europe the soil has been cultivated continuously for hundreds of generations, especially on the Mediterranean coast. This

soil is spent; that is, it lacks trace elements and organic material. And on top of this excessive use is the erosion, which long ago took off the organic horizon and the top layers of soil. In these zones, the only useable soil that does not require fertilizer is found along rivers and in recently cleared forested areas. The rest of the land requires extensive fertilization each year.

The nature of the soil

Kneel down and pick up a handful of earth. You will probably have to use a small spade. Observe if the soil is sandy or very fine, like dust. Sandy soils, which are formed from granite, do not retain moisture well and lack many necessary elements to feed plants, as is the case with the sands on the beach or the banks of mountain rivers. Clay soils, which form from the decomposition of slate or limestone, can be more or less fine. Since all extremes are bad, very fine clay soil has the opposite problem:

The size of the particles

According to their diameter, types of earth are classified as:

- **Rocks and gravels,** which depend on bedrock and which do not form part of usable soil for plants, except to aerate it.

- **Sands,** which measure between 2mm and 50 micrometers (thousandths of a millimeter).

- **Silt,** between 50 and 2 micrometers, and a very fine fraction, of less than 2 micrometers, called clay.

they retain moisture for a long time and not all plants can thrive in this; what's more, when they dry they become very hard and impede the growth of roots.

In greater or lesser proportion, soil is composed of the following elements:

● **Sand**, formed by the decomposition of the parent rock, granite, gneiss, or slate. Granite is formed by grains of quartz and mica cemented with feldspar. When this dissolves with the movement of water, the grains of quartz and mica are freed and carried off by rivers, deposited along their beds, or accumulated on beaches, where later they will mix with other sediments to create fertile soil.

● **Siliceous clay**, formed from the decomposition of silicates in the parent rock, for example, the feldspar from granite. They are typically aluminum silicates and follow the same process as sands, although since they are finer and can dissolve in water, they often go farther.

● **Limestones**, generally calcium carbonate, come from the decomposition of the parent rock, dissolve, and are carried off by rivers to lakes or oceans, where they are deposited on the bottom and harden into limestone rock. When they decompose in the environment, they form part of the soil.

● **Iron oxide**. Come from the decomposition of mica and certain iron silicates, and give the soil a red or yellow color.

● **Salts**. In addition to silicates and carbonates, in the soil there are phosphates, nitrates, and sulfates that come from the decomposition of organic material or that are put in the soil by bacteria activity, like the mycorrhizas of legumes. The phosphorous, nitrogen, and sulfur that plants use comes from these salts, although sulfur is only necessary in very small quantities and excess is harmful. The chlorides that come from the sedimentation of saltwaters are not usually useful to plants.

Original soil with three horizons, A, B, and C.

Eroded soil without the organic horizon.

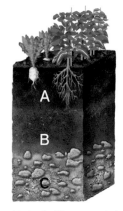

Ideal soil with a composted organic horizon.

In the top drawing, you can observe the three classic horizons, or layers, of soil: an organic A horizon, a transitional B horizon, formed by inorganic materials, and a C horizon, which is composed of parent rock. In the center image, you can observe an eroded soil, without an organic layer, and in the lower image, ideal soil with a deep horizon of compost.

● **Humus**. Comes from the decomposition of organic material, and we will talk at length about its composition in the following sections.

Formation

A virgin soil covered by forest or jungle is formed by a series of well-defined layers, which are divided into an organic part (horizon A) and a mineral part (horizon B), on top of a rocky substratum (horizon C). If you observe a terrain that is recently formed (after an eruption or due to a change in a river's course), you can see how the soil is formed in situ: if the soil is not extremely resistant, it will break up or crack and the first plants will grow in these cracks. **Little by little, in a process that can take years, the soil will grow thicker as an organic layer made up of decomposed plants and the growth** of new ones develops. In flat areas, the soil is usually brought by rivers, which deposit a layer of soil washed down from higher ground, especially at the bottom of the rivers, which, when they change their course, leave fertile grounds uncovered.

If you want the soil of your garden to give you its best, you should add compost or manure regularly.

Texture

Take a handful of soil in your palm, add a little bit of water, and knead it, trying to form a ball. If the ball falls apart, your soil is too sandy. From here, you can determine the grade of the texture of the soil according to your own scale, by trying to roll it out in the shape of a spindle. Continue to roll it into the shape of a fine wafer. If you can do so, you have a clay soil. The four basic types of soil are:

● **Sandy**: The soil will be well aerated and easy to work, but is bad at retaining water and nutrients.

● **Silty**: This is a very fine soil, which compacts easily and can only be penetrated by certain plants. This can be improved by adding a lot of organic material.

● **Clay**: This is a secondary soil, rich in nutrients but excessively impermeable and which, when dry, hardens and impedes the growth of roots. Retains a lot of water and is difficult to work, but can be improved by adding manure or humus.

● **Loamy soils, or balanced**: These are the best and are formed by 20 to 25 percent clay, 30 to 35 percent silt, and 40 to 45 percent sand.

Layers

The soil of our garden, once it has matured and is ready to give yield, will be formed by a mixture of the different horizons that make up virgin soil:

Horizon A formed from organic materials in different stages of decomposition, as we will see shortly.

Horizon B is below the organic material. It is made up partially of primary minerals, in the form of gravel or sand, and secondary minerals, in the form of silt or clay. The secondary minerals, except for humus, have already been mentioned: quartz, silicates (among which is silica), micas, and feldspars (if they come from

Loamy soils have a dark brown color and are extraordinarily fertile; however, industrial agriculture still adds chemical fertilizers, which should be prohibited in our organic garden.

hard rocks such as granite), the elements that form clay (which come from sedimentary rocks like limestone, chalk, or sandstone), and iron or aluminum hydroxides, whose importance is relative until you consider the soils of the Amazon. There, the predominance of iron hydroxides makes the soil harden too much and impede the growth of plants.

Horizon C, which is only of interest if your garden is in the country, or if the soil is shallow enough that you reach it easily, is made up of parent rock. It could be granite, slate, sandstone, limestone, or basalt, among other types. Depending on its nature it will retain more or less moisture and will provide primary minerals. If it is granite, you will have quartz, feldspar, and mica in relatively large grains. Depending on these primary materials, you will find secondary minerals, which form from the biochemical alteration of primary minerals and produce clays and free oxides.

The extracting capacity of plants

The roots of plants function like water pumps. They do not all have the same capillary strength, defined by the ability to take advantage of moisture. **There are plants and trees that need water periodically and in abundance, and prefer sandy, well saturated soils** (where water can be seen). This is the case of the silver fir (*Abies alba*), which needs a lot of water, but also periods of dry soil. **On the other hand, there are species that need water constantly**, like the weeping willow, and which also have a great capacity to extract water from silty (extremely fine) soils,

which retain water for a long time (in the form of invisible molecules) but don't allow all plants to use it. Weeping willows (usually on the bank of a river or lake) grow better in dry places with silty soil, where they can get water every day, than in wet areas with sandy soil, which dries out between rains.

Horizon A

This is made up of fresh organic material, which comes from dead plants and leaves in different stages of decomposition, the final one being humus, which is useable to plants. The process to get to this point is called humification.

Humus is most abundantly formed in temperate forests, where the leaves fall each year. Humification can be more or less active, depending on the climate, which determines the types of bacteria, fungi, and animals present to accelerate decomposition. In forest soils, humus accumulates year after year depending on the amount of fallen leaves, and thus, depending on the type of forest. Beeches are sometimes called the mothers of the earth, because they grow easily and rapidly increase the depth of the soil, but other trees such as oaks, ash, chestnuts, or bananas also have the same effect. In the Mediterranean climate, the holm oak produces excellent humic soils, but decomposition is very slow due to the lack of moisture. Depending on the type of trees, the soil can be acidic or basic, or even unusable, like that created under a eucalyptus.

Humus can be of many different classifications: there are less active and active ones, rapidly formed, divided into acids, carbonates and andics, over volcanic ash, or deeply formed. In all types you will find humic compounds which carry out the decomposition.

Living organisms in the soil
From smallest to largest:

● **Bacteria**: Unicellular organisms that live in soils with a lot of nitrogen and low acidity, around the roots of grasses and legumes, and especially in the rhizosphere. These break down cellulose and sugars and oxidize ammonia into useable nitrates; some are nitrogen-fixing

Porousness

This is the percentage of holes over the total volume of soil, which gives the volume of air and water that the soil can absorb.

The gaseous exchanges that occur in the soil between oxygen and carbon dioxide (oxidation-reduction) are what make the soil useable for plants and allow the roots to breathe. If there is no oxygen, there is no life.

Some willows and purple moor grass are able to survive a lack of oxygen by taking it in through the leaves, and sending it to the roots.

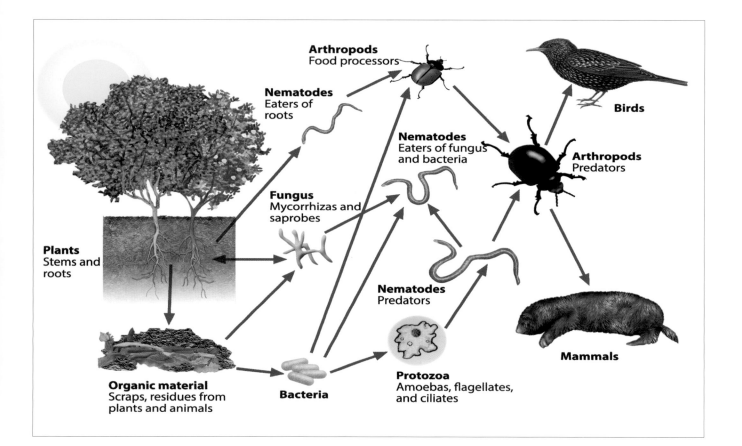

Fungi are extremely varied and contribute notably to humification.

Humification

In the prairies or in the tundra, the soils are formed from the decomposition of roots, which thanks to cold winters, renew each year, producing very deep humic soils that are sold for use in gardens and flower pots. **In agricultural soils, humification depends on human intervention**, with the addition of manure, compounds, straw, grass, dead leaves, compost, etc. which is precisely what you are going to prepare at home.

and others live in the rhizomes of legumes. In swampy areas, there are anaerobic bacteria that provoke methane fermentation.

● Fungi: These are parasitic plants that live on decomposing organic material. They are characterized by mycelia, a system of branching filaments with which they nourish themselves. They resist acidity and drought better than bacteria. There are many varieties. They decompose fresh organic material and cellulose, and hydrolyze lignins, so their action is a necessary step to humification.

● Fauna: This group is composed of the microfauna, including protozoa and nematodes that attack microbial flora; mesofauna, up to 1 cm in size and includes smaller arthropods such as mites; and macrofauna, larger than 1 cm, especially earthworms, but also insect larvae and larger arthropods, especially in acidic soil. The mechanical labor of ants is also very important, since it carries soil to the surface. Termites, on the other hand, interfere with biochemical processes.

Depth

Soil that is less than 32 inches deep before hitting bedrock is considered rather shallow. In Spain, except for in the flat lands, deltas, and some coastal zones, the majority of soils do not reach this depth and the parent rock is easily found. Soils that are deeper are more fertile, and this is observed especially in trees, which grow much higher. If you buy a lot on rocky soil and you want to add some, you must be sure to get alluvial topsoil, although this means we are robbing Peter to pay Paul. Soil that is more than 20 inches below the surface is poor quality and lacks life. You will have to fertilize it, and it will take a while to get a good yield from it.

Natural cycles

The chemical elements essential for life are nitrogen, phosphorous, and potassium, and each one has its own natural cycle.

The nitrogen cycle

Nitrogen is found in the atmosphere in gas form. Symbiotic bacteria that live in the roots of certain plants (legumes, algae, lichens) introduce it to the food chain. The bacteria live on these plants and provide them with useable nitrogen (in the form of nitrates), which transform into vegetable proteins and feed animals. When plants and animals die, the nitrogen returns to the soil in the form of ammoniacal nitrogen. In this way, it is used over again by plants, nitrified by certain organisms (also to be used by plants), or washed into rivers and lakes by rain, where it returns to the atmosphere and the cycle begins again.

The phosphorous cycle

This mineral is found in nature in the form of phosphates, whether it is calcium, magnesium, iron, or aluminum, and gets into the soil through the decomposition of rocks or volcanic eruptions. The phosphate ion is absorbed by plants, which use it to complete photosynthesis. Animals

absorb it through plants and when they die, return it to the soil, where it can be washed into lakes or oceans, or returned to the atmosphere as dust, where it will fall again with rain.

The potassium cycle

This element is essential for photosynthesis and for cells. It is found in clay soils, from which it is washed out by rain. It also passes from the soil to plants, and from plants to animals, and returns to the soil from both. Another necessary element in soil is sulfur, whose cycle has been well studied and is similar to potassium, sulfur appears in nature in the form of sulfates, after having been oxidized from volcanic eruptions. Plants take it up, pass it to animals, and when those die, microorganisms return it to the soil, where it oxidizes and becomes sulfate again.

Trace elements

These are a series of minerals that are only necessary in trace amounts, but are of utmost importance to the health of the soil. These are boron, molybdenum, iron, copper, zinc, and magnesium. They appear as impurities in silicates, hydroxides, or the parent rock.

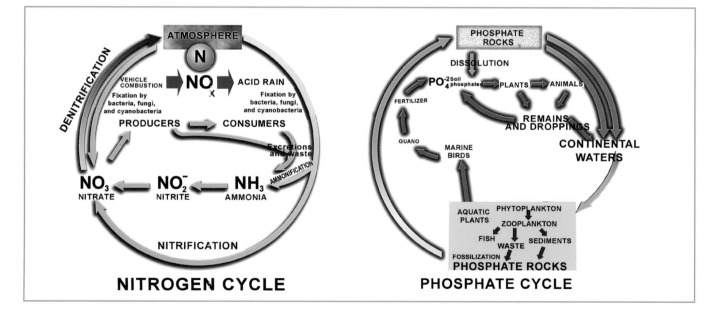

Soils that are frequently washed by rain are usually deficient in water-soluble compounds.

Lack and excess

The lack of minerals, shown in the table below, cause growth deficits, weak plants, and defective fruits. This can happen due to the insolubility of the compounds that contain these minerals, so that even if they are abundant in the soil, they cannot be used. It is possible that you will have to add one of

Lack of nutrients

NUTRIENT	DEFICIENCY
Nitrogen	The leaves will yellow, although there are infestations that give the same symptoms. Its excess will cause rapid growth and weakening.
Phosphorous	The leaves become pale and the edges dry and turn brown. Bears little fruit.
Potassium	Old leaves get reddish, young leaves have yellow or brown borders. Potassium gives the plant resilience. It is often lacking in sandy soils with a lot of rain.
Magnesium	Yellow areas appear between the veins on young leaves, which later affects new leaves. The leaves fall.
Sulfur	Symptoms similar to the lack of nitrogen.
Iron	Like the lack of magnesium, but the yellow stains between green veins appear first on the newest leaves. Often occurs in silty soils.
Zinc	The space between the branches becomes shorter and groups of yellow leaves appear. The old leaves turn golden and fall.
Manganese	Like iron deficiency, but with a green halo around the nerve.
Copper	Yellow stains appear on the leaves.
Molybdenum	Like nitrogen, older leaves turn yellow.
Boron	The plant struggles to grow.

these minerals to your garden to improve its health. The effects of excess minerals are the same. For example, the leaves of the fir that grows on granite of the Vosges Mountains accumulate magnesium, which impedes reproduction because it is toxic to the seedlings. An excess of copper can also occur as a result of sulfation.

How to adjust acidity

The acidity or basicity of the soil depends on the concentration of acidic or basic ions that it contains—in other words, its capacity for oxidation or reduction. A neutral soil, with balanced positive and negative ions, is not reactive and is acceptable to the majority of plants.

pH is measured on a scale from 0 to 14. A pH of 7 equals a neutral substance in which the acids and alkalines are balanced. A pH between 0 and 7 is acidic. To give some perspective, the pH of stomach acid, which dissolves foods, is 1.1, and that of Coca Cola is 1.5—enough to dissolve a piece of meat and surely any plant, since plants can't live in a pH lower than 4 or 4.5. A pH between 7 and 14 is alkaline. On the extreme end

Charlemagne and rotation

During the Roman Empire biennial cultivation was the commonly practiced method. The land was divided in two parts. The first one was cultivated and the other one was idle. The following year the assignment was inverted. **Population growth and careless practice of this system wore out the land in the late Middle Ages**. To avoid this, Charlemagne introduced the triennial rotation, which consisted of two years of cultivation and then an idle time for the third one. Thus, cultivation took up ⅔ of the properties: one year was devoted to cereal, the following legumes, and the third the land was allowed to rest.

Another way of looking at pH

Pour vinegar or diluted hydrochloric acid over a soil sample in a glass and observe what happens:

● **If a strong effervescence occurs, the soil is alkaline and has a pH higher than 7.5.** You should take measures to neutralize it. Copper, iron, manganese, and zinc will be hard for plants to assimilate in these conditions. Add iron sulfate to the soil along with some iron chelate to lower the pH and ease the iron chlorosis in the plants.

● **If it produces light effervescence**, with very small bubbles, the soil is neutral.

● **If it does not cause any bubbling**, the soil is acidic and does not react. It will be difficult for the plants to assimilate calcium, magnesium, molybdenum, and phosphorous. Raise the pH by adding lime.

Hydrangeas are a good indicator of soil acidity. In acid soil, their flowers are blue and in basic soil, they are pink.

Acidity and plants

The preferred pHs of plants

pH	Plant
5.5-6.5	Eggplant
5.5-6.5	Melon
5.5-7.5	Cauliflower
5.5-7.5	Corn
5.5-7.5	Garlic
5.5-7.5	Parsnip
5.5-7.5	Pumpkin
5.5-7.5	Tomato
6.0-7.5	Green beans
6.0-7.5	Cabbage
6.0-7.5	Peas
6.0-7.5	Spinach
6.0-7.5	Sunflower
6.5-7.5	Artichoke
6.0-6.7	Fennel
6.0-6.7	Sage
6.0-6.8	Cilantro
5.5-7.0	Potato
5.0-7.0	Parsley
5.5-7.0	Carrots
5.5-7.0	Cucumber
5.5-7.0	Pepper
5.5-7.0	Rhubarb
5.8-7.0	Endives, escarole
6.0-8.0	Asparagus
6.0-7.0	Broccoli
6.0-7.0	Celery
6.0-7.0	Green onion
6.0-8.0	Leek
6.0-7.0	Lettuce
6.0-7.0	Onion
6.0-7.0	Radish

of basicity is concentrated caustic soda (lye). Be careful with the bleach, sodium chloride, which can dissolve dirt and plants but can't live with a pH higher than 8. It is natural for plants to have preferences, since there are those that prefer acidic soils, such as rosemary, azalea, and hydrangea, and those that prefer alkaline soils, such as thyme, marigold, or petunia. To test the acidity of the soil, you must buy pH testing paper in a drug store or lab supply store. Dilute a sample in tap water, shake well, and insert a strip of test paper. The pH is then shown by comparing the color that appears on the paper with the sample card. Generally, the papers are tinted with phenolphthalein, which turns blue or green in basic soil, or red in acidic soil. Basic soils are those that are high in limestone content—calcium carbonate—with a pH higher than 7. It begins to be dangerous when the pH is greater than 8.5.

Acidic soils are those in which the pH is very low, between 3 and 5. These lack calcium, do not absorb nutrients well, and

do not decompose organic material. They form on slate or granite bases, and in forests with pines or eucalyptus, due to the decomposition of the leaves. It is easily corrected by adding lime until you reach an appropriate pH. In the high regions of the Venezuelan Amazon, some rivers have a pH of 3–3.5 and the water is clear and lifeless.

The life of plants in a vegetable-flower garden develops in soils with a pH between 4.5 and 8. In general, the best range is between 6 and 6.9.

Deficiencies and pH

Alkaline soils tend to lack iron, manganese, copper, boron, and zinc, so many plants such as hydrangeas or oranges will display yellowed leaves. To lower the acidity, you can add acidic peat or powdered sulfur and mix it with the earth. You can also add iron sulfate or iron chelates if you grow acid-loving plants. If the soil is acidic, it will have a deficit of calcium, magnesium, phosphorous, molybdenum, and boron, but an abundance of iron, manganese, and zinc. Correcting this is easy, since all you have to do is add lime.

Chelates

Chelates are used in agriculture to provide trace elements or micronutrients when the soil is lacking. Although it's unlikely that you will use them on a small-scale garden, it's always useful to know the products that are used in horticulture to balance overused soils or ones that are too alkaline.

On the market you can find chelates of iron, boron, magnesium, manganese, molybdenum, copper, and zinc for the garden, but also chelates of amino acids of the same elements that are fit for human or animal consumption, to make these essential elements easier to absorb. Chelates are made with a chelating agent, that is a Ethylenediaminetetraacetic acid (EDTA) that makes the nutrient more easily absorbed by the plant. And not just this, but it also makes the element present in

The difference between sulfate and chelate

Sometimes, in order to promote the absorption of iron from the soil, it is not necessary to add a chelate, which can be very expensive. **If the problem is that the soil is too alkaline,** adding an iron sulfate is sufficient to reduce the pH in the soil.

Iron sulfate is sold in powders. It should be diluted at a ratio of 3 grams per liter of water and sprayed on the ground. This will be sufficient.

the soil more easily assimilable. These compounds, which are sold in vials that should be diluted in water, can be applied to the roots, by spraying the ground, or directly to the leaves, and are notably effective when the plants show early signs of iron chlorosis—yellowing of the leaves while the veins remain green.

A well composted soil does not need any chemical additives to be fertile.

Lowering the pH on the balcony

If you are growing in flower pots or planters, **forget about chelates and even iron sulfates,** since it is unnecessary and, if you mistake the dosage, could make the situation worse.

Normally you would start with a base with a balanced pH, but if you need to lower it because you want to plant hydrangeas in the pot with tomatoes, add citric acid to the water. It is sold in drugstores and looks like sugar. **Another more expensive option is to use vinegar.** In any case, proceed with caution. An option for medium-sized gardens is to use sulfur, or less ecological peat, which has a pH of 3.5.

Care of the Garden

What you need to know about
caring for your garden

Here you face the gardener's most important task: the preparation of the ground and how to maintain its fertility.

Long before any known human civilization existed, since humans discovered or invented agriculture, they trusted the productivity of the land in the hands of a goddess of fertility.

In the beginning, the fertility of the land was one with feminine fertility; this is the idea behind the tiny goddesses with round bellies that our ancestors buried in the ground to ensure a good harvest.

The disappearance of the matriarchy corresponds with the appearance of masculine gods, such as the Egyptian Osiris, that assume, among other things, the fertility of nature. Amulets representing these gods were also buried in the soil.

The Greeks, who are our cultural ancestors, worshiped Demeter, goddess of the fertility of the earth. She was sad because her daughter had to descend to the underworld for four months of the year, and thus is the cause of winter and of rain with her tears.

We don't believe in agrarian gods, because our civilization stopped believing in divine intervention, but we believe in the pleasure obtained from a job done well.

The fertile soil that you want

When you visit an old garden and see the soil, crumbly and dark, which sinks when you walk on it (although you shouldn't do this unless you are working or picking), you hope that your future garden will be just the same, that you will merely have to bend

over and bury the seeds or plant the seedlings, add a little water, and wait for them to grow.

You don't think about the work that is behind that soil, or of the gardener who has been digging, fertilizing, cleaning, mulching, sowing, weeding and picking the fruits and dry plants to return them to the soil in the form of compost.

And if you think, do you do this for the pleasure of the feel of the earth, the pleasure of using the correct tools, of creating a work of art with furrows and rows, in sowing as you should, and the immense pleasure of knowing that "in this soil, two inches deep is enough," in knowing how much water to use and how many days to wait?

Because, is there any greater pleasure than coming to the garden in the morning to find the bright skin of the tomatoes, peppers like mirrors, radishes like fists, and carrots so big that even the rabbits wouldn't attempt it? Stop dreaming and keep reading.

The nature of the soil you are dealing with depends on the climate that has eroded and modified it, and the use it has had previously.

The tools

Although you only need a few tools to maintain a small garden, the simple sight of a series of garden tools, clean, organized, and lined up ready to use, can be an inspiration or motive to get to work. At least you should know which tools you can count on.

The mattock

The size of the mattock that you will use will depend on the size of your garden. For a balcony, you will only need a handheld two- or three-pronged weeding hoe, a small rake, and a spade. You will also need a gardening broom, which looks like a small rake with the teeth separated like fingers.

There are kinds of mattocks and hoes that have two prongs instead of a blade, in case the ground is harder. This will help dig the soil in a small garden, but if you have a larger garden planned, you will need a wheel hoe, which consists of an interchangeable plow applied to a wheel, with handlebars to guide and push it. Of course you could use an old-fashioned plow pulled by a horse, ox, or cow, but this type of plow is beyond expectations for an affordable garden that does not require too much work.

The proposed mattock has a series of blades that can be combined, like a plow, to turn the earth, a scraper to remove the

The basic tools

● **Mattock**: Instrument formed by an iron blade on one side with a sharpened edge on the other, affixed to a pole. It is used to dig and gouge the soil.

● **Hoe**: Similar to the mattock, but it only has a blade on the end of the pole. It is used to pull and push the earth.

● **Rake**: Formed by a long arm with a row of points like teeth. Functions to collect grass and dead leaves, or to smooth the ground after it's been dug up.

● **Pitchfork**: This is a long pole that ends in two or more long spikes that is used to move straw or, in most cases, to turn the soil.

● **Wheelbarrow**: This is a small cart with a bucket to transport a load, with a wheel in front, two handlebars to steer it, and two feet in the back to hold it upright.

● **Watering can**: This is a container made up of a reservoir with a tube and a mouth with numerous small holes, to water plants or freshly sown seeds. You must use this generously.

● **Pruning shears**: These are small, strong scissors that are used to prune trees and strong stems, or, for example, cut the stakes that hold the tomatoes.

Getting home in the afternoon and going out, armed with gloves and a tool, to clear your garden of weeds.

grass between the rows of crops or cover the seeds, to break up the earth and soften it before sowing, and also to bury the seeds, all consisting of a variety of iron spikes that are arranged one after the other at various distances apart.

It would also be a good idea to have a harrow, to open up the furrows to plant seedlings, or to irrigate.

The two-handled pitchfork

As the name indicates, this is a pitchfork with two handles. It functions to aerate and loosen the earth with minimal effort, since it can be forced in with your foot and moved back and forth with your hands to soften the ground. It can be used after the wheel hoe, to soften up the soil where you walked, or simply to aerate it. And in order to get maximum benefit, it should be made of unpainted iron.

Good advice

"In reality, once you've dug the plots or readied the pots, you don't need many tools to work and maintain the garden, maybe a small hoe, a trowel for transplanting, a weeding hoe, a rake, and not much else, since the ground will remain soft since you are not walking on it, and most work can be done simply by hand, which allows for greater contact with nature and life."

Mariano Bueno

The rototiller

The use of a gas rototiller is not recommended for an organic garden. It makes the work easier, but it also pollutes the environment, from both the exhaust fumes and the noise. A gardener who prides himself in his work does not want to find oil stains in his garden.

If you don't have a lot of space, or have a bad back, a good solution is to build work tables with borders a hands-width high. Once filled with soil, you can use them as a nursery, although there are people who use them as a garden, because of how easy it is to water. You can find on the market planting tables of galvanized steel, with a drip irrigation system installed.

Weed whackers and rototillers

There are those who have a yard as well as a garden and buy a weed whacker, one of those tools with a gas motor, an arm that is about 5 feet long, and a disc or nylon cord that turns to cut weeds. It serves to maintain small patches of grass, clean weeds from the edge of the woods, and to cut the grass in corners, along fences, or along walls where you would otherwise have to use pruning shears. It has the serious downside of the noise and pollution it produces. Another thing is the rototiller, which also pollutes and makes a deafening noise. It works well for the small gardener with too much land to dig up by hand, but be careful, because these tools should not be necessary for an ecological garden.

Machines that use gasoline should never enter into your organic garden.

Fertilizer

There are fertile soils that barely need fertilizers, such as the loamy soils of the American Corn Belt, or the volcanic soils, but even these, which produce abundant harvests year after year, need to be supplemented. The plants grow at the expense of the soil and the nutrients they extract from it, making it poorer in quality. So there is no other option than to replace them.

On the other hand, a well fertilized land will be spongy, retain moisture in the right amount, and requires little work to handle it.

Plants take the basic components of their nutrition—carbon, nitrogen, oxygen, and other bioelements—from the air and the soil. In nature, these are replaced when the plants die and decompose. But in the garden, the majority of the dead vegetation is removed to make compost, or because it is diseased. The biogardener should replace these elements by incorporating nutrients into the soil. There are various ways to do so, with organic and inorganic fertilizers.

Difference between compost and manure

Manure has long held a prime position among fertilizers used in agriculture. But from a biological perspective, it's important to point out that manure only enriches the soil when used appropriately. Manures have a cycle of maturation. It is not the same when fresh as it is when mature, or semimature, and its application has different uses. The gardener tends to spread manure from cows, horses, birds, or pigs on their garden, believing it will enrich the soil. What many don't realize is that, buried without oxygen, it will not decompose and its components will not be released; it will just rot and not fertilize. Fresh manure is recognizable by its strong ammonia odor; you can tell it is sterile because nothing grows on fresh manure until it has reached adequate maturity.

Unlike manure, compost has a much more appropriate use in the practice of biologic gardening, whether you have extensive croplands, a modest garden, or a microgarden in the city, such as balcony gardens, flower pots, flower beds, and rooftop gardens, etc.

How to make compost

It is important to choose the location carefully, so that it is favorable to the growth of microorganisms. Compost needs moderate heat and moisture. A spot that is partially shaded by trees will protect it from excess sun and keep it fresh.

It is important to protect the compost from atmospheric extremes, such as heat, cold, and wind.

To block the wind, you can use a fence, ornamental bushes, sunflowers, or corn. If you use a metal fence, you can plant lavender and nasturtium around it, which repel ants and look nice as well. The size of the corner you will dedicate to compost must be in accordance with the area you have available and your fertilizer needs.

Humus mineralizes (becomes usable to plants) more quickly in sandy soils and more slowly in clay soils; heat, working the soil, and organic contributions also help.

Prevent ants from infesting the compost

During the cycle of decomposition, **biocomposters are a very attractive place for ants due to the quantity of nutrients and heat that they generate.** To prevent them from moving in, it is good to plant nasturtium and lavender around. It is a natural repellant.

On the rooftop or balcony, you can use barrels, bags, or sacks with slots or openings that allow air to circulate, although you can also make a small silo out of wood. It is best to have at least two containers, to put fresh scraps in one while the other container ripens, and thus have compost in different stages of decomposition. Once you've chosen a spot, it's best not to change it, since the process gives life to all sorts of living creatures, which inoculate the new compost with bacteria and fungi.

Ideal plants for compost

At first, you can add all the weeds you pull to the compost, but there are two that are especially good for it: **nettle and comfrey**—the nettle because of its richness in nitrogen and in enzymes that support microbiotic life, and comfrey for its richness in minerals, nitrogen, and potassium. Both can be used to make a very useful compound for spraying on the soil.

Natural humus

In the country, humus forms from the fallen leaves and animal droppings. The top layer of dead leaves, branches, and fresh organic material cover the lower layers and accumulate. In the second layer, or layer of decomposition, bacteria and fungi begin to act by attacking the cellulose and lignins of the hard parts—aided by slugs, snails, beetles, mites, and springtails. In this layer, the humus begins to appear; it has a brown color and crumbles in your fingers. The third layer is in contact with the soil and this is the humus itself. Here fungi and bacteria flourish, and it is the territory of the earthworms. You can no longer distinguish the elements of the forest and it has a dark brown or black color.

The carbon-nitrogen balance

Compost needs an adequate mixture of both elements, since an excess of nitrogen accelerates decomposition but produces little humus, and an excess of carbon produces the opposite effect. High levels of nitrogen are found in chicken manure, nettle purine, grass, legumes, coffee grounds, and kitchen scraps. High levels of carbon are found in sawdust, straw, peat, branches, and leaves. Fresh nettles, sheep or horse manure with straw, leaves of fruit trees, and small branches cut in spring help maintain a good balance.

The Four Seasons of Compost

Summer
Work on filling the compost bin. Cover each layer of scraps with leaves and already decomposed material. Dig and stir the pile often.

Fall
Gather the finished compost. Use it as a cover for your flowers or garden.

MATERIALS RICH IN CARBON
Dry leaves
Wood shavings
Sawdust
Branches

MATERIALS RICH IN NITROGEN
Plant, fruit, and vegetable scraps
Animal manure
Egg shells
Tea leaves
Coffee grounds

Spring
Time to start again. Empty the finished compost into the garden and start a new pile.

Winter
Continue making the compost in the cold months. Add kitchen scraps to the compost bin.

Aeration and watering

The majority of microbes need oxygen to survive and carry out their functions. For a compost to develop properly, it needs to take in oxygen and let out carbon dioxide. Therefore, you should choose a place for your compost that is well ventilated, and this depends on the volume of compost. In a terrace, it may be enough to put holes in the bag or drum. In a small garden, use slightly separated boards or wire mesh, and monitor the moisture, which is another important aspect of good compost development. If it dries out too much from too much ventilation, you must compact it, or cover it with a tarp or plastic. If you have a large mass, you can air it out with a compost aerator, pushing it in and moving it back and forth.

The moisture depends on the components. Manure typically doesn't need help, kitchen scraps and plant remains sometimes need straw to prevent excess moisture, but leaves and branches may need watering—in the case of branches, you can even soak them in water before adding them to the pile.

Heat and acidity

Although the small compost piles on terraces or balconies barely see an increase in temperature, if you make a pile of more than a cubic meter, which happens if you have a garden with a lot of trees, the temperature can reach more than 122°F after the second day, and remain at about 140°F for two weeks. At this temperature, the thermophilic microbes work and parasites and undesirable seeds die. If it does not heat up, it's because it lacks volume, it is too dry or too wet, or the carbon-nitrogen balance is off.

As far as acidity, on average it should be more basic so that the fermentation is adequate: between 6 and 8 pH. If it is more acidic—that is, if there are too many dry pine needles, for example—the bacteria

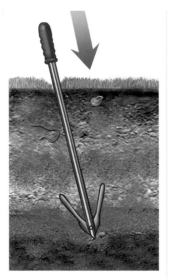

A compost aerator is a tool that is used to introduce air in the compost and thus speed up its decomposition.

al any which way; it's best to have a plan. It's better to have a spot reserved for pre-compost, where you will separately accumulate the fresher elements, such as grass clippings, garden waste such as rotten tomatoes or bean plants, and kitchen scraps, and another to put drier elements, such as clipped branches, straw, or dried weeds. If you have a lot of trees, you will need a third space to collect dry leaves. The pile should be about five feet wide and about the same height, although it can be as big as you want. First of all, you have to create an aerated space for the base, so it's best to use woody materials, such as branches, corn stalks, or dry grass, all ground or crumbled. If the pile is very large, it is good to put aeration tubes in horizontally, or rolled wire mesh forming tubes up and down.

and earthworms will not appear. In a balanced and slightly basic compost, when fermentation happens it releases organic acids that acidify it slightly. However, the final maturation of the compost produces a final alkalinization, leaving you with humus with a pH of 7.5.

The addition of rock dust

In unbalanced soils, either excessively lime-filled or siliceous, it may help to add rock dust to compensate the acidity or alkalinity. But instead of adding it directly to the soil, you should add it to the compost. For example, limestone soil can be corrected with compost of clay or loam, and clay or acidic soils can be corrected with limestone rock dusts, like dolomite, lime, or natural phosphates.

Ways to make compost

There are two ways to get a good compost for a small garden: the pile and the container. The compost pile is the easiest to prepare, because you just need a space to accumulate the waste.

Experience shows, however, that it's not enough to just accumulate the materi-

The progressive pile

In many cases, a small garden does not allow you to make huge compost piles which produce decomposition with an elevated temperature. They are progressive piles, to which the gardener adds scraps continuously as they come. In this case, one should mix them with a pitchfork every time new material is added.

From there, alternate layers of about 8 inches thick of fresh, fine materials with thick, dry materials, and between each layer, put a layer of old compost, manure, or previously fertilized soil from the garden. Between each layer you can also add powdered ash, rock dust, dolomite, or whatever element is necessary to correct the deficiencies of the soil.

Each time you add a layer, you should mix the previous ones with a pitchfork. If the climate is dry, you can water it whenever you water the garden, or do so when it has not rained in a while, but it's good to always maintain consistent moisture. It can also be sprayed down with a compound of nettle or comfrey.

When the pile is finished, cover it with a layer of soil and straw, and water it until it becomes compacted. But you can also use other materials, such as tarps or plastic sheets, as long as the sides are uncovered.

Ripening

The compost is at its peak when it has transformed into a brown humus that smells like the forest. If it has been made on top of soil, you will be surprised to see that once they completed their mission, the earthworms disappeared.

To test the level of moisture, dryness, and ripeness, stick a broom handle or cane into the center of the compost. If it comes out black and greasy, this is a sign that it is too wet and could rot. You should aerate it and turn it as soon as possible. If it collapses, it is too dry and could mold. You need to spray it with warm water. If it is ripe, it will have the moisture of a wrung-out sponge.

At the end of a month, in any case, it is good to dig it with a pitchfork to give it a little life. Experts recommend you make compost and stir it when there is a full or waning moon. As we've seen, the temperature will rise to about 140°F for a few weeks, then cool down.

Two or three months later, it may already be useable as fresh compost, to mulch, not bury, as long as it does not touch the plants.

Five or six months later, it is ripe compost and can be used to fertilize the soil, and after a year it becomes humus and will no longer evolve any further. This is a good time to make new beds.

Compost containers

In general, these are used when you don't have enough waste to make a pile as we proposed previously. So, you can use compost bins, barrels with holes, or bags in which the organic material is added to the top and the decomposed material is collected from the bottom through an opening.

With a certain quantity of compost but not so much space, you can take advantage of a wall or build large boxes, in which you will add compost as previously described. It is best to have two boxes made with boards or bricks, which get higher as the pile grows. In one, you will deposit fresh organic scraps, and in the other you will collect decomposed compost. If you have space, you can prepare three boxes to have compost at different stages of decomposition, but this depends on

The decomposition of leaves

It is faster if the leaves come from fruit trees, maple trees, ash trees, lime trees, banana trees, or chestnut trees. **It is very slow if they are hard leaves such as those from beech, poplar, oak, or walnut—these should be ground before adding them to compost.** Pine needles require special treatment: one week in water, three weeks of fermentation, and three months of ripening before they can be used.

Bokashi

This is a Japanese compost that is being used a lot in Latin America, and has the advantage of fermenting in as little as 15 days, after which it is ready to use. Its essential components are:

- chicken manure
- carbon
- rice hulls and ground rice
- cane molasses
- yeast or humus from the forest, or already made compost
- soil
- calcium carbonate or lime
- water

the preferences of each gardener. Don't forget to make it the same as a pile on the ground, alternating layers, mixing, watering, and adding mature compost or manure.

Manure

The traditional fertilizer that has been used since the beginning of gardening. When a small landowner or someone who has just bought a farm decides to make a garden, the first thing he will do is ask the nearest farmer for a load of manure. By adding this every year, the soil will never wear out.

In regions with poor soil, watering with purines, which are nothing more than diluted manure, maintain fertility indefinitely; however, its excessive use in areas with lots of livestock, especially pigs, is common and this pollutes wells and rivers, and the rain washes the excess nitrates into the groundwater.

It's not always possible to choose the type of manure you want, since it depends on what is available. If you have the choice, in a dry climate, sheep or goat is best, and in a wet climate, cow manure is best.

Sheep and goat manure

This is very concentrated and its direct application can burn the plants; however, it's good for making a balanced compost. In any case, it's best to let it age a year, like chicken manure.

Cow manure

Ideal for wet soils, this can be used directly or in compost, although you have to watch it because it tends to have a high water content.

Pig manure

This is widely used on large tracts of land in the form of purines. By itself, it is very thick and tends to harden. It is not good, however, because it usually contains antibiotics and other chemical substances used to treat the pigs, or to fatten them.

Horse manure

Considered very good, although it is weak for making compost, since it decomposes quickly. It tends to have a lot of cellulose because it comes mixed with straw from the stables, and once it has fermented it loses its odor. It is used in starter pots and seedling beds.

Rabbit manure

This is too strong and acidic to use directly. It should be mixed with compost and complemented with lime or dolomite to cut its acidity.

Chicken manure

This is the manure of any domestic birds. It is too strong to use directly, since its components pass rapidly to the plants. It is not unusual to find a hobby gardener who has burned her plants with chicken manure applied directly to the soil. If you do so, you will have to wait until the next year to get a good yield, although it's best to add it to compost or prepare with the bokashi that is shown on the previous page.

Dead leaves

If your house has a path lined with deciduous trees, you will collect a huge quantity of leaves in the fall. These leaves, rich in carbon, decompose slowly, and if they accumulate on their own, they quickly compact and ferment. It is good to mix them with other waste, such as ground branches or kitchen scraps, and make a separate pile to make a good peat to add to the compost after winter.

A good way to store them is in a ring of wire mesh, staked to the ground. This way they will be aerated and under control, for example, from the wind.

Biodynamic compost

One of the most prestigious organic farmers in Spain, Mariano Bueno, author of the excellent book on compost titled *Como hacer un buen compost (How to Make a Good Compost)*, tells us: "In biodynamics, one adds different preparations to the compost, the manures, and the liquid manures, to increase their effect on the plants and the soil," since, "the goal is not just to activate the world of the microorganisms, such as bacteria, but primarily to concentrate the vital forces . . . "

In this type of agriculture, cow manure is "the noblest material," and therefore it can be used separately or mixed with vegetable compost.

Fruit fertilizer

In a five-gallon bucket, put two pounds of fruit and two pounds of molasses or honey, in alternating layers. Finally, cover it with wood, or put a heavy weight on top to press it. **After 8 days, filter the liquid obtained and put it in bottles.**

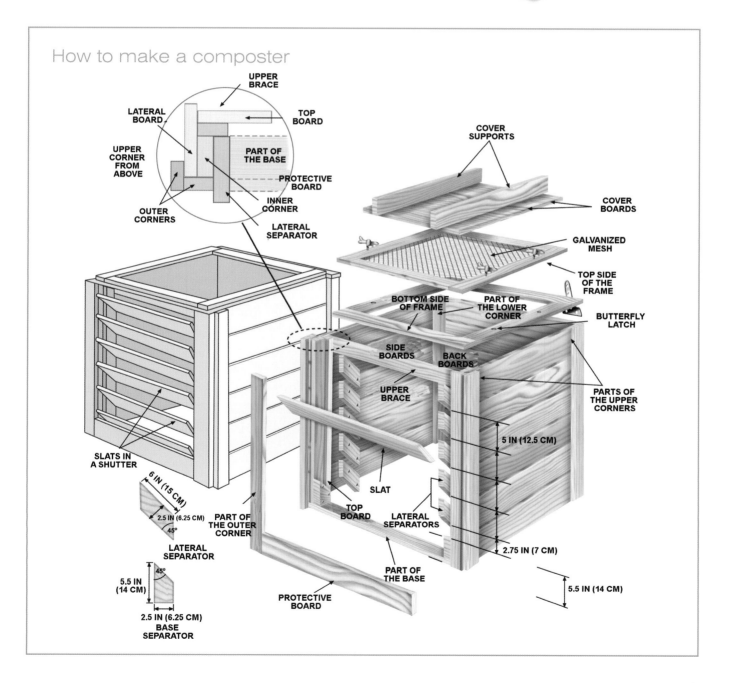

How to make a composter

Solarization

It is recommended every three or four years. It eliminates fungus, nematodes, worms, weeds, and bacteria through heat and asphyxiation. It is not a very humane method, but it works.

This is a technique to disinfect the soil. You must have room in the garden, it requires very little work, it eliminates seeds, roots, and parasites from the soil, and it consists of heating damp soil, using solar radiation, by covering it with a sheet of polyethylene that retains and accumulates heat.

Method

It must be done in the summer, between early July and mid-August, and the steps are:

Deep excavation of the soil—if it is done with a rototiller, adding the subsoiler and then the rototiller, to break up all the clumps.

Measure the width of the plastic sheets and dig furrows at the right distance to bury the edges. If you are using several, you will have to bury the edges in the same trench.

Abundantly water the soil, at least 16 inches deep.

To improve solarization, add fresh manure, which will ferment in the heat and add more heat.

Cover the soil with plastic, so that it is taut and in contact with the soil. If the solarization is done with a tunnel of plastic, it is called double-layered, and will reach even higher temperatures.

The thickness of the plastic depends on the wind, but it should be between 100 and 200 gauge thicknesses.

Leave for 30 to 45 days in full sun. The soil will reach temperatures above 122°F.

Problems

You must keep in mind that the effectiveness is less at the edges, within at

The goal of solarization is to avoid the use of insecticides and pesticides, so sometimes the use of plastic can be justified in a medium or large farm.

least a meter, so it is useless to do this with very small parcels. It is a technique used by growers with a relatively large area of land, possibly near a wild area where animals will tend to confuse the plastic with water and could tear it. In this case, you would have to fence it with a few strands of wire, even to prevent cats, dogs, and chickens from getting in. If you have a tractor, do not drive over the plastic, as the effect will not be the same.

Irrigation

Watering is one of the gardener's pleasures, so never deprive yourself of watching the furrows as water flows through them and reaches the plants, wetting their roots.

In very few climates can you go without watering the land. In the Mayan mountains, for example, seasonal rains occur during the growth cycle on a daily basis, then stop when it's time to harvest. Corn, green beans, and squash are perfectly adapted for this cycle.

This type of planting could also be done in our climates and we will almost certainly get a good harvest, as long as we protect ourselves from the climate change.

Irrigation in dry climates allows you to obtain maximum yield from your crops, but you must be careful to avoid excess water. Some plagues and diseases develop because of excess water and in many cases, you will have to take measures to aerate the soil.

Methods of irrigation

Probably, the first irrigation system was done by flooding, as they still do today in Egypt, where the water is pumped from the channels of the Nile River and poured directly onto the fields. This option requires a huge quantity of available water, and flat fields, but over time produces salinization of the soil. Unless you have a good drainage system, the water accumulates on the surface and evaporates, depositing salts that will turn the soil unproductive. If you don't have that much water available, the best option is furrow irrigation. The plants are planted on ridges separated by furrows that can be opened or closed with a hoe. Since the water can go as far as you want from the main channel, it is possible to irrigate on slopes by making terraces.

All you have to do is open or close the furrows to water the plants that need it and when they need it. The same way, the furrows can be lined with a hose connected to the water source or siphoned from a pond. A more sophisticated system of irrigation is by sprinkler, installing a hose and sprinkler that can be turned on when needed. This system, similar to watering with a hose from the edge of the garden, is good for onions, leeks, and carrots, or other types of crops on flat ground, without furrows. However, there is the risk of wetting the leaves too much, which favors the growth of fungi.

Drip irrigation requires an initial investment that, in the case of industrial plantations, is amply compensated through the conservation of water in areas where it is scarce.

Drip irrigation

The best option that is currently out there is drip irrigation. This system, however, is a huge step back from our idea of a self-sufficient garden that requires very few tools. It is most advisable to water with channels or, if you have a pond nearby, by channeling the water through furrows, although it requires daily work. Drip irrigation is designed for large gardens or those in which the farmer is frequently absent. If you have a weekend garden, this system is suitable, but first you must be willing to make the initial investment, and maintain it.

The eternal watering can

Never forget this tool, which is so useful for watering seed beds and seedlings that have just been transplanted. It is the best option for small tomatoes, peppers, eggplants, etc. And you can always decorate the watering can to your taste.

Filling the watering can in late afternoon and sprinkling the beds, making sure the watering is homogenous and does not damage the fragile, newly sprouted plants is one of the best ways to get in touch with nature.

For larger areas, it's better to use a hose and even the hoe and irrigation channel, to let the water run and feed that which will be your sustenance the next morning, when the peppers and lettuce are ready for the healthiest, most delicious salad you can imagine.

The system

Drip irrigation consists of a system of hoses that goes through the whole garden with a small hole next to each plant for water to come out. The irrigation is programmed and, in each section, the garden should have an electric valve that opens and closes when the programmer decides; this way, we can program different routines for tomatoes and eggplants, for example, without leaving home.

Ideally this water would come from a source positioned so that the pressure is always the same. If it comes directly from the faucet, before the electric valves you should install pressure regulators and filters to avoid obstructions. In the holes of the hose, put drip emitters, which can be of different kinds. You will also need elbow, 4-way, and T-tube fittings to connect sections of the hose. If the hose if very long, you will need auto compensators to maintain the water flow at the same pressure.

The average flow for drip irrigation is one gallon per hour. Under each plant there will form what is called a wetted zone—narrow and deep in sandy soil, and wide and shallow in clay soil.

Frequency and problems

Obviously these plans are not applicable to all plants, but fruit trees, for example, should be watered according to this plan: in spring, three or four times a week, for about 20 minutes with a flow of one gallon per hour; in summer, daily, for at least half an hour; in fall, five to ten minutes two or three times a week; in winter, depending on the rain. As you have seen, this system is good for fruit trees and flower gardens especially, although it is also used in large gardens where the ridges are covered with plastic. The system is ecological at first, but anyone who has seen these types of crops, with the plastic hoses (made from petroleum) piled up each year at the end of harvest, with hundreds of meters of broken tubes or those destroyed by pollutants, will not be too attracted to this method. It

Climate change is causing shortages of rainfall in many areas where not so long ago, it was common. Although alterations to the climate are normal throughout history, the increase of carbon dioxide causes a more precipitous change. One way to avoid it is by planting trees, since forests favor rain and prevent excessive heating of the soil.

certainly saves a lot of water, but that is not the idea we have of a garden. Watering should be done depending on the needs of the plants. And you have to be there to see with your own eyes and to feel with your own senses.

The forest and the microclimate

Advice for watering

● **Water in the early morning** or at sundown.

● **Avoid the hours of most intense sun**, although if it is cloudy and cool you can water then.

● **Don't use water that is too salty**, since except for tomatoes, all plants will weaken quickly. If the water you have is too salty, use tap water.

● **Make sure the water is not too hot or too cold.** The ideal is that the irrigation channel, if you have one, is well shaded by trees.

● **Keep in mind that the wind dries the soil** and that, if you have

a wall to protect it from the wind, the sun will still dry it. Each garden and each parcel has a different history, and finding that out is one of the pleasures of gardening.

● Tomatoes, peppers, green beans, squash, peas, and cucumbers **need more water when they start to flower**.

● **Root plants**, such as carrots and beets or radishes, need more water when the roots are forming.

● **Leafy plants**, such as lettuce and spinach, must be watered frequently before they ripen. Otherwise, they will bolt quickly.

Excess watering

If you waste water in the garden, the only thing you will achieve is causing moisture that attracts fungi and other diseases, as well as causing the fruit to lose flavor. Tomatoes and carrots that are overwatered become bland, and then you can't complain. Some people are too impatient, or enjoy watering so much they want to do it every day; sometimes you must contain yourself.

Plants should be watered when they need it, and if possible, you should distribute the plants to fully take advantage of the water. You must also keep in mind that plants need more water when they are young, and when it is almost time to harvest, you should stop watering, so they get more flavor. You must also consider that root crops, such as potatoes, when overwatered, produce a very tall plant (as when it rains too much) and very few tubers, which is not what you want.

The best yield

To not waste water, it is best to make sure the soil is conditioned to retain it, without puddling. Sandy soils, for example, retain very little water, and are good for certain species like ash, which want to have water only when they are thirsty. On the other side of the spectrum, clay soils retain a lot of water and rarely get muddy, but when water is scarce they do not give it up to the plants and only some, such as the weeping willow, are able to extract it from the capillaries of the earth. To avoid these problems, we use organic material, which contain water and oxygen together. But you already know that a good fertilizer solves these problems.

The emitters

The hoses used for drip irrigation will have holes every 12 to 16 inches in which there are drip emitters, through which the water comes out. These can be button emitters, which are stuck into the hose and can be taken out, or integrated, which remain fixed along the hose. You can also use a drip irrigation tape or even a hose with holes.

In flower gardens, the hose is often buried, so you have to install some microtubes from the hole to the surface, where you will attach the emitters.

One foreseeable problem involves the lime in the water, which ends up obstructing the emitters. Experience teaches us that the best emitters are those that can be removed to be cleaned. Cleaning is done by sticking a needle in the holes to open them, or with diluted nitric acid, taking necessary precautions.

Proper **sowing**

The importance of
proper sowing

The first and most important thing that the self-sufficient gardener must do is obtain the proper seeds, and then treat them with care.

Let's not fool ourselves, without good seeds, there is no worthwhile garden. The majority of the seeds that our grandparents used have disappeared from the market, and only exist in the hands and cupboards of a few old gardeners and lovers of good food, who guard them like a great treasure. So in order to begin, we must behave like detectives, and then we will learn to use them.

Seeds

Plants reproduce through seeds. The embryo of the new plant, its form and characteristics, are all contained inside a seed. The job of the gardener is to select the best seeds, from the best plants or fruits, so that the new generations are better each time. It is always said that you should save the best tomato from the first crop for seeds. That is how your biologic garden should work: with your own seeds, selected each year, at least for the majority of the plants, although it's not always possible.

Many of the seeds that are available commercially are hybrids; that is, the companies that produce them have crossed incompatible plants through force so that they are more resistant and have a greater production. The seeds obtained from these plants are not the same and will not work for the next year's seedlings. So, if you buy them, you have to be very sure that they are not hybrids.

The selection of good traditional seeds, in the face of the surge of genetic technology by the agro-industrial companies, has become a real battle. It even feels somewhat radical.

In just a few days, all the plants in your seedbed will have sprouted. Then you will have to thin them, so that they don't get in the way of each other, and get rid of the weakest. If you take a little dirt with them when you transplant them, it will be easier for them to take root, although if you have them too close together you won't be able to. In some cases it is even good to air them out a little, such as with lettuce and onions. Want to know a trick? Mix the seeds of radishes and carrots. The radishes grow more quickly and save you from thinning out the carrots.

Let's experiment

Some schools ask children to perform the following experiment with vegetable seeds: disinfect them with diluted bleach and put them in boxes with cotton and pieces of damp cloth, keep in the dark, and wait for germination, which will have occurred in most of the seeds at the end of a week. Start with the fastest, the radishes, and continue with squash and pumpkins, onions, spinach, peas, green beans, cucumbers, leeks, chard, eggplants, peppers, tomatoes, and carrots. As soon as the plants have sprouted, they should be transplanted to pots or other containers in which there is potting soil, not soil from the garden.

Some specialists recommend covering the container (open milk cartons, cups, pots, or whatever) with transparent plastic. This way, they maintain heat and speed up germination.

When the seeds have sprouted, you have to thin them carefully, and when they are two or three fingers high they can be transplanted to bigger containers, although many gardeners prefer to leave them in the original container until they are big enough to transplant outside.

The method can be great if you have children, because it allows you to observe germination and note the time each species takes, but be careful: this is not the best method to grow seeds that you are going to plant in the garden. Those should develop from the start in a layer of soil, and if they are going to be transplanted, it should be done as close as possible to the final location, so they adapt. For this, instead of wet cotton, you can use potting soil in pots and then place them directly in the spot they will grow. Don't use peat, since a cubic meter takes five hundred years to develop, and it's a resource that has been excessively plundered.

The largest known seed is that of the Sea Coconut, *Lodoicea maldivica*, and weighs 44 pounds (20 kilograms). The smallest belong to the epiphytic orchids, and there are almost a thousand million in a single gram.

The quality of the seeds

Experience will teach you which are the most useful seeds, but to start, use those produced by the best fruits from the first crop, and let them dry on a paper in the shade.

If you buy seeds in envelopes, keep in mind the following factors that should appear on the back of the package: the germinating power (as a percentage)—that is, how many of the seeds from the package will germinate; **the longevity, which indicates how long the seeds will have germinating power** (remember that once exposed to air, some will not last more than a year); and the purity, which indicates the proportion of seeds in the contents of the envelope.

Onion seeds have the shortest germinating power; they cannot be kept for more than a year. After them are **parsnips, dandelion, spring onions, sweet corn, peas, leeks, green beans, lima beans, and parsley**, which barely last two years. The rest begin to weaken after the fourth year, up until the ten years that endives and cucumbers can last. Don't trust any seeds that have been in an envelope for more than five years. In order to lengthen the duration of the fertile state of the seeds, put them in a tightly sealed glass jar and keep in a dark place.

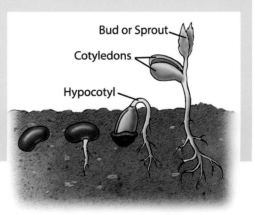

Bud or Sprout

Cotyledons

Hypocotyl

Forms of reproduction

Reproduction through seeds is just one of the ways that plants have to propagate themselves; for example, no one ever thinks of planting potatoes this way. Here we see some of the possibilities.

Seeds

This is the universal method. The plants grow, flower, and the flowers transform into fruits that contain seeds. Some, like cacao, have a germinating power of a few days, while others, like baobab, have a germinating power of a few years. The seeds of gymnosperms are very resistant and can wait long periods of time on the ground. The sequoia needs fire to open the seed, while other species need to be soaked for several days. In general, (moderate) heat and moisture are enough to cause germination.

Cuttings

Some plants, such as rose bushes or many fruit trees, can reproduce by cutting a young branch and planting it in the ground. In Guatemala, I have seen walls built by cuttings that sprouted in the spring, producing colorful flowers. In general, this occurs with species of softwoods, in which the sap runs close to the surface and can flow with a small scratch. Cuttings are also sometimes called slips.

Suckers

Similar to the previous case, but these are branches that grow very close to the ground and have their own roots, such as with olives. This system is used with artichokes in the garden.

Runners

Some plants project horizontal stems a specific distance and, once in contact with the ground, these grow their own roots, and from there sprout leaves and a new plant, which can be separated from the mother plant and transplanted to another place. The most common example of the use of this method is with strawberries, but water reeds also reproduce this way.

Bulbs

Some species, like garlic and onion, or tulips, form bulbs at the base of the stems in which they store nutrients that help them sprout again the following year. **To use them, separate the shoots from the original bulb, store in a dry place, and plant them separately the next season.** This does not mean that they don't grow from seeds, but by using the bulb you will avoid having to plant in a seed bed and wait more than a year, except in the case of onions, since the bulb does not last that long.

Layering

Like the previous case, but forced. There are two main types: air layering—in which you make a cut in a branch, cover it with peat, and wrap it in plastic until it grows roots—and ground layering, in which you bend a branch and bury part of it underground, tying the part that comes out to a stake, like with a vine. Once the branch has sprouted and grown roots, it is separated from the mother plant and transplanted. (See Fruit trees).

Tubers

These are roots that store reserve substances and form enlarged bulbs, from which a new plant will emerge, as occurs with potatoes, sweet potatoes, yuca, begonias, and dahlias. The way to use them is to cut them in pieces and plant them separately. With flowering plants, the reproduction of tuberous plants is better done with cuttings. As is the case with bulbs, reproduction through seeds does not allow you to maintain uniformity of the species as using the roots does.

Rhizomes

These are underground stems that grow horizontally and put out shoots, which allows us to separate them to reproduce the plant. This occurs in canes, bamboos, ferns, and water hyacinth.

Grafts

This consists of joining part of one plant to another. Then it begins to grow and you have a new plant formed from two different ones. It is a curious form of reproduction widely used in fruit trees.

Uncovered seedbed

In gentle climates, where frost is rare, such as on the Mediterranean coast, you can sow directly into the soil. The first condition is that you've prepared a small parcel of land with the best soil possible: the organic substratum that you've prepared.

In some gardens, it's not unusual to find even old buckets in which there is a mess of disorganized tomato and pepper plants growing, which the gardener will use to substitute those that die off. So an open air seedbed can be made on the ground, in boxes, in buckets, in a wheelbarrow, in pots, or in beds. In the same place that you already did the protected sowing, it is common to sow an uncovered bed later to replace the losses.

Protected seedbed

Any of the previously mentioned forms of constructing a seedbed can serve as a starting point. It is enough to just cover it with plastic, which will heat the ground and accelerate germination. If it is on the ground, put stakes in the four corners to hold up the plastic, and if you have planted in rows, you can put metal hoops and make a greenhouse tunnel, although I'm not fond of this industrial option since the use of plastic implies pollution. You can also put

What can we plant in the seedbed?

Although depending on the climate, you can plant in a covered or uncovered seedbed, the plants that need to spend some time in protected soil free of weeds and parasites are **celery, eggplants, onions, cabbage, lettuce, pepper, leeks, and tomatoes**. In greenhouses, they also do this with melons, cucumbers, and watermelons.

resistant glass over it, which can be taken off easily, or put the pot on the windowsill or simply put it on your porch.

The hotbed

This is a seedbed with its own heat source, which accelerates germination and protects the plants from the cold. It is made by forming a series of layers in the seedbed: the first serves as drainage and is mainly gravel; the second formed by manure, mainly horse manure since that is the one that produces the most heat; a third of old compost; and a fourth of humus, in which you will plant the seeds. All of this goes under a roof. The manure should be moist and compact, although not too much or it will not ferment properly. If you do not have horse manure, make a mixture of sheep and cow manure. A simple pile of dry leaves, buried more than two feet deep, begins to heat up quickly. With manure, it does not need to be more than 8 inches deep.

In ten or twelve days, the temperature in the bed will be 140 or 160°F, but you must wait until it goes down to 75°F on the surface before sowing. You don't want to exterminate your own seeds.

Planting in containers

In this modality, the seeds are placed in small containers such as those sold in the market or in greenhouses for transplanting. If you do this at home, anything works, from an egg carton to ice cream boxes or ice cube trays. Fill the container with a mixture of sand and compost, wet it, and make a hole with your finger or a small stick, and put a seed in each hole—a couple if they are very small. Cover with glass or transparent plastic to retain heat and keep in a warm place (for example, on top of the fridge). The next step is to leave one plant per section, when they have two or three leaves, or separate them about two inches if you are using a wide container.

Repotting

This is done when the plants have two leaves. Prepare another tray with one part organic substratum, one part mulch, and one part sand. If you don't have a tray with containers but just a flat one, it's a good idea to make a board with nails distributed at regular intervals which you can place on top of the substratum to mark the spots where you will put the new plants. Stick a sharp pencil or stick into the place where you are going to transplant and insert the plant, without bending the stem. There are wooden gadgets you can buy in the shape of a 'V' to avoid touching the plant with your fingers, although a fork works as well. With the same pencil, pat down the soil around the plant.

Water the soil generously, without wetting the leaves, keep in the shade for a day, and then put in a place with abundant light, but out of direct sun.

Don't bury the transplanted seedlings with the roots folded and the ends facing up. This will make the plant do unnecessary work and they will take longer to grow.

lettuce, onions, celery, and leeks because this will make them stronger. Place them in holes made with a stick, taking care not to fold the roots.

The influence of the moon

It has always been believed that the moon has a certain influence on plants, and so old gardeners keep this in mind when it comes time to plant. There is no doubt that the attraction the moon exerts on the earth has a certain influence on all the phenomena of the biosphere, most notably the tides. Plants clearly reflect the action of gravity, since this determines the direction that they must grow in. It has been shown that plants that grow without gravity do so randomly, in no particular direction, and tend to self-destruct.

We must observe the moon from two different points of view. In one, we consider the lunar phase: whether it is waxing, full, new, or waning. In the other, we consider if it is ascending or descending on the horizon, since during the period of time when we see it in the sky, which lasts 28 days, it appears at first higher in the sky each night, and then, lower each time.

These two phenomena must not be confused, since sometimes there is a waning moon that is ascending at the same time. The moon is ascending when it is moving to the north toward the constellations Aries or Taurus. And it is descending when it is moving south, each time lower in the sky, and gets nearer to Libra and Scorpio. The cycle lasts about 27 days.

The phases of the moon, on their part, last a little more than 29 days, depending on the illumination. It is waning when it appears like a C and waxing when it appears like a D.

Ascending and descending moon

The ascending moon favors activities with the aerial parts of plants, such as grafting or picking fruit, which will be much juicier. It is unfavorable to pruning, as it will spill too much sap, or planting garlic.

Direct thinning

Some people consider thinning to be moving the plants directly to the ground. But if you let them grow a little more, until they have four or five leaves, then we can talk about transplanting.

Transplanting

This is the definitive move of the plant into the ground of the garden. Once the plant has grown to the appropriate size, you will have a root ball—that is, the plant with the soil that accompanies the roots. In this case, we can talk about moving the root ball to the garden. If you used containers with individual plants, you will just have to turn them upside down and gently loosen the root ball. Then place each one in the hole you have made in the ground and water abundantly. This is the correct method for tomatoes, peppers, and eggplants, for example. If you do not have individual plant containers, and you have to pull the plant out with the roots and minimal soil—such would be the case for a tray of plants you bought at a store or perhaps a bucket of tomato plants—you will have to move as quickly as possible to minimize the time the plant is exposed, and you will plant it just like those plants that are transplanted with naked roots. It is better to do this with plants such as

The descending moon means the majority of activity is transferred to the ground. This is the time to work the soil, fertilize, and harvest roots such as potatoes, carrots, onions, or garlic. It is also the time to prune, since there is less sap, and to perform other tasks related to the ground, such as transplanting and planting cuttings, since they will take root better. It is also a good idea to chop firewood, as it will dry quicker.

Waxing and waning

When the moon is waxing, the vitality of the plants diminishes, and if the moon is ascending at the same time, it's the ideal time for grafting. The grape and olive harvest is best done during the waning moon, since it is said that the grapes are sweeter and the oil is better. This period is also a good time to plant roots and tubers. The legend that garlic comes out of the ground if it is sown in the waxing quarter is well known, so you should do the opposite.

The full moon, favors the planting of lettuce and the pruning of hardwood trees. On the other hand, they say it is best to harvest aerial crops in the waxing moon and roots and tubers in the waning quarter, except for garlic and onions, which prefer the waxing moon.

Pumpkins and squash must be harvested during the waxing moon, although the truth is that with the oil in the hot pan and the fruit fully ripe, I would not wait too long. Another aspect to keep in mind is **the apogee and perigee of the moon,** that is, the closeness of the satellite

On the left, a **waning moon**, and in the center, a **waxing moon**.

in its revolution around the Earth. It is said that during the perigee, when the moon is closest, it is not good to work in the garden, since its influence is greater. The plant is more sensitive, potatoes sprout eyes easily, etc.

And the planets

The moon has its favorite plants. According to cosmobiology, chard, watercress, melons, and cucumbers are lunar plants. Each planet has its own influences: Mercury prefers plants with fine stems and small flowers, such as anise, parsley, and fennel; Mars prefers conical roots, like garlic, mustard, or nettles; Venus, the most beautiful plants with white flowers, like orchids or thyme; Jupiter, the big aromatic fruits, like cabbage, grapes, figs, or olives, and nutmeg, oregano, and jasmine; Saturn likes trees that live for many years and ancient, slow-growing plants like horsetail, hemlock, holly, plantain, onion, and potatoes. The sun, obviously, prefers plants that reproduce its color and shape, like oranges and sunflowers.

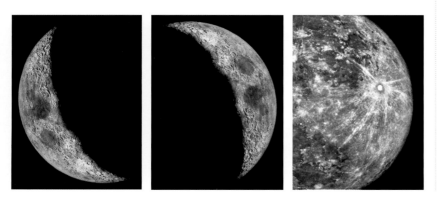

Good and bad
company

Good and bad
company

There are many ways to get rid of plagues that attack the garden without harming the environment or contaminating the foods with chemical products.

Weeds

The gardener's first problem is the problem of weeds, the so-called "bad plants" that for us are simply "annoying." Especially for weekend gardeners, who stay away for five days and come back to find the garden invaded by weeds, there is no other choice than to pull them. There are two types of plants that threaten our gardens:

Annual plants

These are born from seeds and only live a few months, such as the poppy, dandelion, and wild oats. These are easy to eliminate with a hoe, spade, trowel, or by hand, pulling them out when the soil is damp so the roots come out more easily.

Perennial plants

These reproduce by rhizomes, such as Bermuda grass, nettles, bindweed, and Java grass. These require more work, since even if you pull them, pieces of root will still be left behind and sprout again at the first opportunity. But don't despair, keep pulling them and each year they will be weaker, until they disappear. After several years of fighting, I have been able to completely exterminate nettle stalks that seemed invincible, simply by cutting them with a weed whacker over and over again. However, don't let your guard down, since the seeds can always come back on the wind.

Harmful insects

The majority of insects end up being beneficial to the crops, mainly through pollination but also from the aeration of the soil by ants, for example, and the contribution to forming humus and converting certain chemical elements into useable form for plants.

There are, however, a percentage of insects that are harmful because they eat the crops, whether as adults or larvae. Or because they attack the roots and kill the plant. And this population of harmful

Controlling weeds

The best way to get rid of annoying weeds is to not let them grow, by laying good mulch around the crops, which can be straw or wood chips from fruit trees.

But if they are already there, you have to face them. If they are tall, you will have to grab them by the stem, as close to the ground as possible, and pull them out in one go to eliminate the aerial part and as much of the roots as possible.

It's not a good idea to take drastic measures like salting the pathways or the cracks in the pavement. The best thing is mulch, or if not that, proper weeding.

Useful insects destroy 80 percent of harmful insects. The grower only has to worry about the other 20 percent.

A seven-spotted ladybug can devour up to 250 aphids a day.

Earthworms

Earthworms are one of the most cherished species of gardeners and agriculturists, since they allow the soil to stay aerated, and form a layer of humus that enriches it.

Their activity of swallowing and digesting the earth is very productive, since the organic material that they excrete allows for the accumulation of high-quality humus.

Shake a juniper branch in autumn: a few ladybugs that have not yet gone dormant will certainly fall out, and hurry to get back on.

plants proliferates from year to year due to the use of insecticides that leave only the most resistant ones alive—which must then be combated with even more destructive pesticides.

It is certain that science is working toward the creation of more specific insecticides, which only destroy the species, but recent events show that these do not actually work. When they fumigated areas such as the Ebro River Delta to kill off an infestation of insects, even the butterflies ended up suffering. The destruction of harmful and beneficial insects alters the balance of nature, and anyone who has an organic garden must keep in mind that if the garden is near large farms or even pine forests that suffer from processionary moths, it's very likely that large-scale fumigations affect all the insects in the area.

We propose an alternative idea that can be beneficial for all: the creation of an island of beneficial insects, where they can safely take shelter and reproduce.

The beneficials

Beneficial insects are the predatory ones, that is, those that eat other insects. Among them, a standout is the hoverfly, those flies with yellow and black stripes on the abdomen that hover around flowers. Their larvae are big consumers of aphids.

Ladybugs are efficient predators; the two-spotted ones hunt in trees and the seven-spotted ones do so in the lower vegetation, and thus are the ones we see more frequently.

Some species of bedbugs are also beneficial because they capture and kill harmful insects such as red spiders and some butterfly eggs, which hatch into leaf-devouring larvae. Lacewings, with their four transparent wings, are big aphid and mite hunters. Hunting wasps—not all of them sting!—are also useful for plants. Finally, there are the parasitic insects that live inside other insects, such as some worms that—and this is not safe for kids— eat away at their victim but leave the nervous system intact so that it lives to the last moment.

Good plants

These useful insects will look for food and protection in the plants you have put in your garden. As for food, it could come from the sap or molasses of some plants, and for protection, hollow stems can work well, from species such as blackberry, elder, raspberry, or reeds. Wasps engineer those clever hanging houses that cause us so much panic, and will sometimes make them in tubes or even in the keyhole of seldom used doors. The plants that we are going to propose have diverse functions, as nectariferous plants or as refuges for the insects, but they are also decorative and can be wind blocks for us.

Neutralize plagues with plants

Plants don't just serve to attract beneficial insects, but they also repel harmful ones or serve for hanging traps. For example, **garden nasturtium** is used at the base of fruit trees to fight aphids; **cabbage, turnips, and radishes between tomatoes** repel various beetles; **hemp and rosemary** scare off cabbage moths; **Jimson weed** repels moles and **elder branches** stuck in the ground will scare them off; and **parsley** at the foot of rose bushes eliminates green aphids.

Juniper has many uses, since it protects beneficial ladybugs and gives us gin, and is an excellent wood for making kitchen utensils or pipes.

Bocage and open fields

The disappearance of insects is not only due to the use of insecticides: it is largely due to the removal of the vegetation that allows them to survive. A controversy erupted in northern France because of the disappearance of numerous species of birds. **The cause of the disaster was due to the liquidation of the bocage**, which is an agricultural system of small fields separated by strips of vegetation covering the slopes on uneven terrain or separating the plots of different land owners. In these green lines, which when seen from above give the landscape the appearance of a chessboard, some farmers planted fruit trees and medicinal and aromatic plants, particularly in Mediterranean areas. Others simply let the weeds and brambles take over and burned them off every year. Still others grew the trees and shrubs that birds and beneficial insects need to live. Modern agriculture, based above all on performance, and the use of large machines, required the removal of these margins, and the leveling and transformation of the fields in large desolate expanse. This open field system facilitates farming but removes vegetation and the associated wildlife that lives on the margins.

Prevent and fight

A garden in Asturias

The soil is clay and the climate is very wet. To improve the soil, they add ripe manure, which is called *cucho*, to make the soil spongier and keep it from compacting too much. To fight acidity, they add lime each year, and to ensure the peas have enough potassium, they add ash from wood fires.

Plagues, the prevention

Begin by choosing the best plants. You can start with your own seeds, but in many cases you will buy them in a nursery or market from other farmer. Don't buy ten tomato plants to plant ten tomato plants; buy a few more and select the healthiest ones after planting them. If you plant one that appears sick, is yellowed, or has few roots, you will most likely have to replace it.

Select the species

Think about the climate and soil in your garden. It's not the same to have a garden in one region of the country as it is in another, or in a tropical country. Peaches, cabbages, and onions need cold; tomatoes need heat. If your garden is at a high elevation, the growing cycle will be shorter and later. Potatoes will flower later. There are some species of tomatoes that grow well at 1500 meters above sea level in the Pyrenees. In this case, it's best to buy your seedlings in a local nursery or market, or grow your own from the first and best specimens of the previous year. If you buy seeds in a different city, do your research. Another important question is the soil in your garden. If it is well conditioned, you can plant anything, but if it is new land, you will have to factor in the acidity and salinity, as well as the consistency. Peanuts require very loose soil, and chickpeas don't care as much. Root plants also need loose soil to grow well. Salinity may be caused by excessive watering or being close to the coast. Look at the tables included in the chapter on soil to see how well different plants resist acidity.

Condition the soil properly, as we explained in the section on soil, with the pH within a healthy range and the necessary drainage. Avoid contaminated soil. You can also disinfect it via solarization with a layer of coconut fiber.

Don't forget about rotation

To avoid wearing out the soil, you know that you can't plant chard in the same place for at least two years. Keep in mind that every garden has areas with better sun or more wind, and this depends on the trees, walls, or buildings that are around it. There are species that don't tolerate wind and need to be sheltered. Try to give the tomatoes full sun. Green beans don't need as much light, although they still need some. Cucumbers and squash wrinkle with too much heat and are fine if they get shade in the mid-afternoon. Your own experience will teach you the assets of your garden. Try to space out the plants and form combinations that will help each other mutually.

Biologic warfare

Biological plague control consists of the use of the natural enemies of the infestations to finish them off. The use of chemical products such as pesticides, herbicides, and fungicides is prohibited. The pollution they cause is well known, as well as the appearance of resistant species and the harm to human health caused by the consumption of chemically treated foods.

Biologic warfare that is practiced in greenhouses or large plantations follows these steps:

- Identify the attacking species.
- Figure out what its natural enemy is.
- Quantify the damage caused or calculate the population of the attackers.
- Calculate how many specimens of the natural enemy you will need.
- Obtain the natural enemy and encourage it to intervene.
- Test the effectiveness of the method, without losing sight of which is the attacker and the attackee.

These methods are not as fast as chemical products, and require more hours of work. The use of natural enemies is also delicate.

In our small garden, we don't have the luxury of these methods, although it's not a bad idea to learn about them. Ours will be a team fight. We will plant the proper plants, use our hands, and water the plants with mixtures that you will see shortly. This is the time to meet the enemy.

Surround the garden with aromatic plants, such as lavender, rosemary, salvia, and thyme, which help to avoid insect invasions and can always be used to make soup or tea.

Bad company

The majority of these **unwelcome visitors** are found habitually in any garden, although you shouldn't consider them invincible or too destructive if you give them proper attention.

Birds

At one time, sparrows and corvids were considered plagues, since they descended upon recently sown fields of grain in vast flocks and devastated the fields. They can be fought off with scarecrows, nets, shiny paper, plastics, or CDs that are hung to move in the wind.

Cats vs. Dogs

Depends on how they are trained. **Both dig, urinate, and defecate.** Cats are more predictable: they like to roll around in freshly dug earth, in which they also do their business, digging up and disturbing the seeds. If they are young, they will play among the lettuce, cabbages, and seedlings, breaking anything in their path. But they also protect the garden from birds and moles. You must evaluate the pros and cons, but in general, cats are not your enemy. There's also not much you can do, since as soon as you are not looking, they will go back to what they were doing. However, some people recommend transparent water bottles, since the reflections of the sun seem to scare them off. Dogs are more particular, since there are many different breeds and characteristics. **In general, small dogs are as annoying as cats and barely scare the birds.** Big dogs might squash plants, but you can train them not to go certain places or dig, and that is enough. You can also give them a sandpile for them to do their business, and teach them to do it there.

Rabbits and mice

- If you have your garden near a forest, you will be visited by rabbits that eat carrots and all sorts of green plants if you don't put a three-foot fence around your garden. Since cats eat the baby rabbits, they are effective for controlling the rabbit population.
- Mice are easily combated with a cat or with traps (do as you like, but we don't endorse kill traps).

Moles

If you have moles in the garden that dig up your fields, feed a cat. Felines are very patient. They like to sit and wait for hours for a mole to appear that they can hunt and play with. Remember that jimson weed also repels them, and if you pierce their tunnels with elder sticks, they will leave your dominion. Some use traps, ingeniously engineered from wire, at the entrances to their tunnels, or hang balls with camphor to scare them off. Voles, which are smaller, feed on bulbs and roots. Place camphor or mothballs in their tunnels. Ultrasounds also work, and they sell traps that don't harm them. Moles are more abundant in wet years, since very dry earth is difficult to tunnel in.

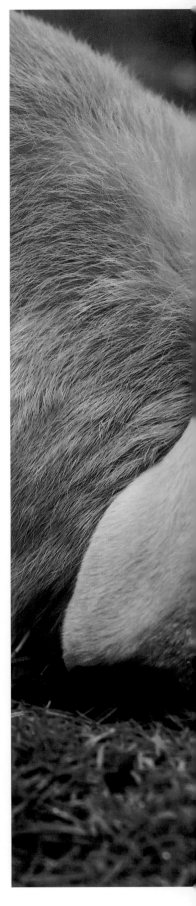

Snails and slugs

Both flourish in wet areas. In rainy years, they are a good food source. All you have to do is get up early and collect them before they eat the tender leaves of newly sprouted plants.

When there begins to be too many, you will have to resort to other methods. Among the ecological options are:

• Place bricks or up-side-down containers to give the snails and slugs a place to hide from the sun. If you also include orange peels, it will be easier to catch them in the morning.

• Place a plate or tray, filled with beer up to the rim, so that the snails climb in and drown. Some people attract them with lettuce leaves or slices of potato.

• Scatter shavings or ashes around the plants so that the snails don't pass over them. When they get wet, you have to replace them.

• A cruel method consists of breaking up eggshells and sprinkling them around plants. They catch the slugs and snails and they die.

• Snails also have predators—toads, ducks, geese, and hedgehogs—which can be your good friends in this sense.

As a method of prevention, only work the soil superficially, since slugs take shelter in deep soil; don't spread out compost but mound it, and don't leave the soil in clumps since they also like that. In winter, you must dig up the eggs so that they freeze.

On the other hand, some species of slugs are useful for the decomposition of vegetable scraps.

Ants

The ant should not be the enemy of the organic gardener. In fact, lately they are in decline, as if they were one of the insects harmed by mass fumigation or climate change. However, ants bother us because they favor aphids. They carry them up the shoots and collect the nectar that they secrete. They are often found on rose bushes.

They also gnaw away at recently sprouted plants and steal small seeds. It is not surprising that the carrots disappear before sprouting. Ants are, in general, beneficial, since they attack the caterpillars in trees. But if you don't want them to get out of hand, you can make a funnel from paper and fasten it around the tree. The ants, while ascending, will have to go down and this will throw them off. If you also place cotton balls with a sticky substance, you will end their plans.

Other possible systems are: put salt in their path, put soapy water at the entrance of their holes, spray a nicotine solution (not recommended anymore), trap them with honey or sponges soaked in sugar water, or use lemon juice, which they don't like.

It is also common to lime the trees, grease them, put a circle of cotton strung on a wire, or put sulfur around the base.

Finally, it is possible to plant a series of plants that repel them, such as lavender, mint, thyme, marjoram, marigolds, etc. And in the garden, they also dislike lettuce, so look for similar plants.

Worms

There are many types: the click beetle worm (Agriotes lineatus), and white worms (Anoxia villosa) are found by digging up the soil with a knife to find the damage to roots. Cutworms (Agrotis segetum) eat the base of the stems.

● Click beetle worms are attracted by fresh manure and can be trapped by burying slices of carrot or potato. Once captured, cut them in half.

● Cutworms attack the stems and leaves of new plants. They are found by digging up around the plants that you find wilted each morning, or looking for them with a flashlight at night, although the best way to eliminate them is to dig them up in winter.

● White worms are the larvae of the violet carpenter bee, and they attack strawberries, lettuce, and artichokes. They should be fought by finding them in the soil or following the method described for cabbage moth caterpillars.

Above: the click beetle **worm** (*Agriotes lineatus*), fierce attacker of roots, is the larvae of this inoffensive-looking beetle.
Below: root of lettuce attacked by **nematodes**. In bio-gardening, it's common to plant certain species that repel them, such as *Targetes patula*, *Schkuhria seneciodes*, *Ambrosia trifidus*, and hybrids of helenium and gaillardia.

Nematodes

Nematodes are very small worms, less than 0.2 millimeters. They live underground and attack bulbs and roots, and the only way to discover them would be to send them to a laboratory. They like sandy soils, heat, and humidity.

The most common variety leaves small lumps on the roots that can be detected by pulling them up. The plant gets weak or wilts little by little. The fight against these worms is complicated, but in ecological agriculture you shouldn't bother with them too much. In any case, if you begin with a soil infested with nematodes, the best way to get rid of them is solarization.

Potato beetle

Mole cricket

They are 1.5 to 2 inches long and they cut the roots of plants when they are still young and tender. The name of the mole cricket comes from its digging legs, similar to those of moles, which feed on these insects.

You must defeat them by catching them, and the best way to do so is to bury empty pots level with the soil so that they fall in. Another system is to make holes and fill them with manure in winter to trap them little by little.

In summer, they can be discovered when you dig up the earth and find the tunnels they make as they go along. You can flood the tunnels, or poison them with rotenone. Some people place a mixture of two tablespoons of coffee, a few oleander leaves, and a few cigarette butts diluted in water at the entrance of the tunnels.

The best way to get rid of beetles is by picking them off one by one by hand, but not everyone has time for this, and it's not reasonable if you have a lot of land. Chamomile planted between the potatoes will repel the potato bug and it is a lot less work.

Its origin is in the United States, to the east of the Rockies, where two centuries ago they devoured all kinds of thistle and barely bothered the potatoes that grew wild in the mountains. Once the extensive cultivation of potatoes with inorganic fertilizers began, the beetles began to attack them. But the real problem began when, in the mid-nineteenth century, North American farmers began to spray the potatoes with lead arsenate, the first known broad spectrum insecticide.

Instead of eliminating the beetles, it made them stronger and eliminated the rest of the fauna, among them, another predator beetle, and bees and birds that fed on them. In the mid-twentieth century, the potato bug was already a worldwide plague. Today, the only biological way to fight them is picking them by hand or planting chamomile.

In the search for a biological remedy that can be sprayed on the fields, they are studying species such as *Bacillus Thuringiensis*, of the subspecies Thenebrionis, which has proven effective in the control of the beetle, but with the danger that resistant larvae will emerge, making the cure worse than the disease.

At the time this book was written, they were attempting to isolate the toxin that this bacillus contains that kills the beetle larvae, to incorporate it in the genetic fabric of the potatoes, and create a dangerous genetically modified product with toxins incorporated.

Aphids

This is one of the most common plagues. There are many varieties and they attack almost all plants. Plant louse, as they are also called, can be seen with the naked eye, because the leaves of the plant appear curled up, or from the yellow stains that their bites leave. The black aphid is accompanied by ants that graze on it, collecting drops of honeydew that the aphids excrete, formed from the sap that they suck from the leaves.

The apparition of the insect

Aphids are born fully formed, since they are viviparous. The females may have wings and are the ones that spread to other plants. They can transmit diseases if they bite a sick plant and then a healthy one. They are very adaptable and mutations can occur in a single season.

They often appear due to a poor management of the garden. Above all, it is a surprise if they go a week or two without showing up. When you fertilize too much or add nitrogen to the soil, it increases the sugars in the sap and the plant oozes or bleeds, attracting aphids, which will reproduce quickly.

The remedy

● **First of all**, keep the garden clean between the plants. When there are weeds, they propagate. As soon as the aphids appear, you must remove the affected leaves. Gardeners suggest using a toothbrush on plants with flowers to clean them.

● **You must attract the natural enemies** of the aphids: ladybugs and wasps, or parasitic wasps that increase vegetable diversity. Earwigs are a natural enemy that you can help with a few tricks (see the section on earwigs).

Signs of the presence of aphids

● **They are visible to the eye.**

● **The leaves curl at the tips.**

● **Yellowish bite marks appear on the leaves.**

● **Sooty mold, a fungus, appears, which can be fought with copper oxychloride.**

Rose bushes can be attacked by green or yellow aphids. If you don't want to get rid of them by shaking the leaves, you can use a solution of pyrethrin every fifteen days, a natural insecticide obtained from the chrysanthemum flower.

Natural enemies of aphids

In the biologic warfare that greenhouses use to fight aphids, you will find two parasitic wasps (*Aphidius ervi* and *Aphidius abdominalis*), **a midge larvae** (*aphidoletes aphidimyza*), **and a lacewing** (*Chrysoperia carnea*). The **wasps** lay eggs inside the aphids and the larvae eat them from inside. The **midge** lay eggs nearby, and when they hatch, the larvae crawl toward the aphids and empty them by suction, as do the lacewing larvae. To get an idea of how these battles work, let's look at the case of the **lacewing**. The grower can buy a few boxes that have a hundred eggs each and hang them over the affected plants. They can also be purchased in the form of larvae mixed with rice hulls, and you just have to sprinkle them around.

- **Also to prevent them,** you should avoid excessive fertilizer, sow at the right time, and water when needed, to prevent the plants from oozing, which attracts them.
- **Spray slightly soapy or warm water over the leaves,** with some pressure from a hose to wash them off.
- **Use an infusion based on nettles.**
- **In trees,** it's enough to just hang some sticky tapes to trap them.
- **You must control the ants,** since if there are too many they will protect the aphids that give them honeydew.
- **Concoctions of wormwood,** walnut leaves, tomato sprouts, or garlic are preventative treatments.
- Curiously, **a light sprinkling of very fine dust** will finish them off, since it dehydrates them. And in this vein, some gardeners lay aluminum foil around the plants so that the heat dries them out, although be careful since this can damage the leaves as well.
- **The use of natural insecticides** like rotenone or pyrethrin in late afternoon will help.

The Wooly Aphid (*Eriosoma lanigerum*)

White in color, it attacks fruit trees and appears in groups on the trunks, branches, and twigs; can be combated with a few dabs of alcohol. It is also effective to mist the trees with nasturtium extract. A sprinkling of lithothamnium will dehydrate the aphids.

- Sodium silicate three times a year will successfully fight off aphids in fruit trees:
- In winter: a 3 percent solution.
- Before the buds sprout: 2 percent solution.
- On the leaves: a 1 percent solution.

Of course, the water that you use in all these preparations, if it is possible, should be rainwater or spring water. This will double the benefits of the preparations.

Flea beetles

Flea beetles are coleopterans between 2 and 3 millimeters in size, that lay eggs on the stems of plants, and whose larvae feed on the roots. They attack potatoes, cabbages, parsnips, beets, and artichokes. They can be fought with soapy water, aromatic plants, tomato plants, and straw laid out in fall to catch them in winter.

Soapy water, prepared with a little dish detergent, should be used with caution, as it can affect the leaves' stomata.

Red Spider Mites

These are very small mites of two kinds, *Tetranychus telarius* and *Tetranychus urticae*, which have two spots. They vary in color from red to yellow. They have four legs in the nymph stage, when they attack all kinds of plants: green beans, cucumbers, peas, squash, tomatoes, apples, and strawberries. They plant themselves in the underside of leaves and suck the sap from the plant. They are resistant and easily mutate to adapt to attack.

They can be detected by the blotches that appear on leaves, and you can even see the spider webs around the leaves.

The easiest way to fight them is by keeping the plants moist, since they love dryness, so with plants that will tolerate it, mist the leaves.

It is important to prevent mites by keeping the soil clean of weeds and making precise rotations. Excess fertilizer will encourage them.

They are repelled by onion skins scattered between the plants, and to mist the leaves you can use infusions of horsetail, nettles, or wormwood, and if they resist, pyrethrin or rotenone.

The natural enemies used to fight red spider mites are three predatory mites, used in greenhouses.

Thrips

These are very small insects, between 0.8 and 3 millimeters long, that come in various colors and look like miniature earwigs. There are various types and they are found in flowers. *Kakothrips pisivorous* attacks legumes, *Thrips palmi* attacks cucurbitaceae, *Frankliniella occidentalis* transmits a virus, and there are others that attack ornamental plants, tobacco, olives, citrus fruits, etc. Thrips reproduce by eggs and both larvae and adults feed on sap, leaving characteristic white marks on the leaves. The flowers won't open and the leaves will become deformed and fall off. Their presence can be detected by tapping a flower on your palm and letting them fall into your hand. They like dryness and heat, and can be fought with moisture. Avoid weeds and use blue adhesive traps at the height of the plant. The ecological insecticide recommended against thrips is pyrethrin or pellitory. Biologic warfare in greenhouses is done with predatory mites that are sold in plastic bottles with bran to keep them alive.

Leafminers

Leafminers (*Phyllocnistis citrella*) are lepidopteras, meaning that tiny butterflies lay eggs on the tender leaves and stems. The larvae feed on the leaf tissues, excavating tunnels in the interior. Only the dry cuticle remains, making the leaf wrinkle and curl. Heat stimulates them. Leafminers generally don't affect fruit trees too much; although there are other miners of the genus Liriomyza, that attack lettuce, for example, but generally they are only a danger for decorative gardens. They can be fought with pyrethrin, but since they live inside the leaves it is difficult to reach them. The best method is to pick off the larvae by hand. In biologic warfare, they use three parasitic wasps of the genuses *Dacnusa*, *Opius*, and *Diglyphus*.

Earwigs

Earwigs are beneficial to the garden because they eat aphids, but sometimes they build nests in fruit trees or in corners of dry wood and become a real nightmare. To capture them, use flower pots full of straw turned upside down on sticks, or roll corrugated cardboard around a stick at the same height as the plant.

Leafhoppers

Typhlocyba rosae, also known as leafhoppers, are small insects of about 3 millimeters that live on the undersides of leaves and suck the sap. The leaves will progressively become discolored. They are combated in the same way as aphids.

Control insects with aromatic plants

● **Basil** wards off flies and mosquitoes. It is good to put it next to tomatoes, and inside the house you must keep it in a well ventilated place with plenty of light.

● **Borage** attracts bees.

● **Chives** scare off aphids.

● **Dill and fennel** attract beneficial insects with their strong odor.

● **Lavender** repels ants. Especially when prepared as an infusion.

● **Mint** repels aphids and other insects. Don't hesitate to use it, even in an infusion.

● The variety of mint known as **pennyroyal**, and **rosemary**, are used in wardrobes in the house against fleas and ants.

● **Rue**, when crushed in water with a little **salvia**, is also a strong insect repellent.

● Don't forget **thyme**, which attracts bees and repels aphids and cabbage moths.

Diseases

Squashes, as well as pumpkins, cucumbers, and melons, are attacked by powdery mildew from the Cucurbitaceae, which manifests in the form of powdery white splotches on both sides of the leaves, which end up drying out.

Insects are not the only enemies of the plants. There are other smaller ones that require different attention. Bacteria, fungi, and viruses are waiting for their opportunity to attack your garden. Let's meet them and learn how to defeat them.

Powdery mildew

This is a series of fungi that are very easy to diagnose. It is also called white mildew, or white powdery mildew, because it takes the form of a white or ashy powder that appears on the leaves, stems, and fruits. It makes the leaves and stems yellow. The fungi spores are distributed by wind and when they fall on a stem or leaf, they root themselves. Once they have grown, they stay where they are rooted. This develops during wet springs and dies off with heat

and dryness. It attacks all Cucurbitaceae, and in the flower garden, rose bushes, geraniums, laurel, oaks, begonias, bananas, etc.

Fight back by eliminating weeds from the garden, to prevent trapped moisture. It's best not to wet the plants if the mildew is growing, and as soon as you notice it you must pick off the affected area, or pull the whole plant if necessary. Be careful not to spread the fungus all around when you do so.

Mildew

This is a fungus (*Phytophthora infestans*) that appears with moisture and is detected because it first attacks the edges of leaves with yellow blotches, which then extend to the rest of the leaves. These appear brownish and grey mold appears on the underside of the leaves. It also attacks the stems and fruits, and it's not unusual to find it on potatoes or tomatoes that seem to rot before ripening.

It's also known for attacking grapevines and rose bushes. It only develops when it is hot and the plants are wet for several hours at a time.

It is fought by keeping the crops clean with freely circulating air. Once it appears, you can fumigate with Bordeaux mix (contains copper sulfate) or with horsetail, although the idea would be to do it before the disease appears. When it is hot, you can sprinkle sulfur over the plant.

Bacteria

These are not that common, and tend to affect decorative plants more, but they can also affect green beans, tomatoes, and peas. The symptoms are ulcers that can appear up and down the stem and round stains on the fruits. In tomatoes, black splotches will appear on the leaves, stems, and fruits, although they are very small. The bacteria of mange or scabies will also cause black marks and can even produce large pustules in the fruit. And finally, there are the soft, watery rotten spots on tomatoes that give off a bad odor. In any case, if you start with healthy plants and select the best seeds, you won't have problems with this.

Treatment with copper oxychloride works well.

Virus

Viruses that attack plants are transmitted mainly by aphids, but also by whiteflies, leafhoppers, thrips, or nematodes.

The main characteristic of a virus is its resistance and mutability. There is no way to eliminate them with chemical products and attempting to will cause them to mutate. There can be a million symptoms—dwarfed plants, mosaics, yellowish splotches, or tumors on the leaves. The only way to fight them is by eliminating the sick plants, keeping the garden free of weeds, choosing resistant varieties, or

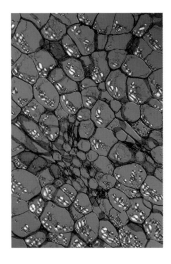

Top: *Phytophthora infestans,* magnified by one hundred. (Photo by Gary Gaugler)
Bottom: A field of potatoes attacked by mildew.

eliminating the carriers, aphids.

You can keep viruses at bay by spraying essences of aromatic plants like lavender, thyme, or rosemary.

Fungi

Fungi attack plants in many different forms: some rot them, others secrete toxins that kill them, and others block light. Ahead, we will take a look at the most common ones.

The mosaics are named for the appearance of the leaves, which take on a colored mosaic of shades of green. Most of the time this is produced by some kind of virus.

White rot

This is produced by the fungus *Sclerotinia sclerotiorum*. It is detected because it forms a white mycelium around the affected parts, which looks like cotton wrapped around the stem of the plant. It is caused by excess moisture and can be controlled by keeping the garden free of weeds and eliminating affected plants.

Botrytis or grey mold

This is caused by the fungus *Botrytis cinerea*. Botrytis starts to produce brownish lesions, then soft rot in the tissues of the plant. It is found in tomatoes when you cut them open and find the grey mycelium of the fungus.

Like the previous one, it is caused by excess moisture and is controlled the same way. It affects plants after they have been damaged by hail or chewed by insects. Therefore, one way to prevent it is to avoid harming the fruits while trimming or harvesting, when you might accidentally scratch the stems. And avoid planting the same species in the same place.

Finally, you can water with nettle broth or wormwood broth.

Sooty mold

This is the fungus that appears on the honeydew that aphids, whiteflies, and wooly aphids excrete. It is named this because it looks like a black powder that weakens the leaves, mainly because it blocks the sun from reaching them. Sooty mold is controlled by eliminating the pests that cause it. Once it appears, mist the plants with soapy water. Some eliminate it from peach trees by planting garlic under the trees.

Alternaria

Alternaria is a fungus from the genus Alternaria, whose presence is announced by spores visible on the affected tissue.

It typically appears on the ground, on dead vegetable material, and in wet spells

Alternaria attacks plants from the soil and spreads on potatoes and tomatoes during wet spells.

can spread rapidly to the plant, which necrotizes and dies in a few days from a toxin excreted by the spores. There are many varieties adapted to different plants or trees that they attack, for example, *Alternaria solani* attacks solanaceae and feeds on the tomato (alternariosis), forming elongated marks and concentric circles on the stems and stalks. It is controlled by keeping the garden clean and preventing excess moisture.

Rust

Rust is a fungus whose symptoms are orangish pustules on the undersides of the leaves and stems. It only appears in cases of extremely moist climates. It is controlled by pulling affected leaves and fumigating with copper, as well as following all the steps already mentioned for preventing moisture, like eliminating weeds and avoiding dense foliage.

Diseases produced by fungi are usually caused by excess moisture, which you can reduce by clearing the mulch and layer of dry plants from the soil.

Anthracnose

It is caused by fungi of the genus *Colletotrichum* and *Glomerella*. The symptoms are well defined brown halos appearing on the leaves, sometimes concentrically like burns. To combat it you must remove the affected leaves and burn them or take them directly to the trash. Otherwise, the spores will return to attack the plant.

Verticillium and *Fusarium*

These "wilting" fungi can be detected when the upper leaves of the plant droop and the lower leaves start to yellow. To avoid infecting nearby crops, remove and burn the diseased plants. Do not add diseased plants to your compost. (Solanaceous plants like tomatoes and potatoes are especially susceptible.)

Blight

What we call blight in potatoes and tomatoes (*Phytophthora infestans*) is also known as potato, eggplant, or tomato smut. That of rose bushes (*Peronospora sparsa*) produces brown spots on the leaves, and corn smut (*Ustilago zeae*) blackens the corn cobs.

Tomato blight is detected, for example, by watery spots on leaves and fruits. It is caused by moisture and can be fought with bicarbonate.

Root rot

There are many fungi that can rot the roots. **Among them are those of the genus *Fusarium*, *Rhizoctonia*, and *Phytophthora*** (image). They are detected because the leaves dry and turn brown. The remedy is in its cause: waterlogged roots by overwatering or in case of rain, poor drainage.

Sunburn

Tomatoes are one of the plants that suffer the most diseases, and also sunburn on the worst summer days, appearing as whitish stains on the skin.

Scarred fruit

These occur when the plant has plenty of water some days and not enough on other days. Cracks appear near the stem.

Rot due to lack of calcium

This occurs at the base of the plant and is not caused by a fungus. It is offset by adding calcium chelates.

Gallery of grievances

After briefly viewing all the enemies of the garden, we classify them with a good science textbook in hand. Let's see the result:

- **Vertebrates**: mammals and birds. Among the former are wild boars, dogs, cats, hedgehogs, rabbits, rats, and mice. Among the latter are all grain-eating birds, although some have a special hatred of corvids, which are not easily fooled by a scarecrow.

- **Arthropods**: insects, arachnids, and crustaceans. Among the former are ants and aphids, among the second group are mites, and among the latter, mealybugs.

- **Mollusks**: snails and slugs.

- **Worms**: white worms, cutworms, and nematodes.

- **Fungi, bacteria, and viruses**: they are numerous, and the smaller they are, the more adapted to the species that they attack.

Keep in mind also that these are not the only enemies we have in the garden, and nature also has something to say, regardless conditions like the following:

- **Lack of light**
- **Sunburn**
- **Excessive heat or cold**
- **Hail**
- **Excess water**
- **Wind**
- **Acidity or alkalinity of the soil**
- **Lack or excess nutrients**

Natural remedies

Running water, especially if it is from a spring, is a good remedy against mites, spider mites, and thrips.

Natural remedies are those that make use of other plants or chemical substances that are accepted by ecological agriculture. We will also comment on more elaborate systems, such as color traps and pheromones.

Mineral oils

To prevent pests in fruit trees, mineral oils are often used in winter and summer. These oils are sold already prepared, they are derived from petroleum, and they are formed from saturated and unsaturated hydrocarbons. They are effective against insect infestations.

Their advantage is that they are cheap, nontoxic to humans, do not create resistance in the insects, and fight all the pests that hide in the trees, preventing them from proliferating. There are winter and summer mineral oils. The winter ones, which will have a milky appearance, are thicker and should be used diluted with water.

They are used when there is a stop in the vegetative cycle, that is, November to December, and you must be careful because they are phytotoxins, which can damage leaves of nearby plants. They fight aphids and spider mites. Paraffin oil should be diluted at a measure of 6 cc (the dose of an espresso is 20 cc) per 10 liters of water, and spray the plants with a sprayer. It should not be used on perennial plants, or at temperatures above 75°F.

Running water

Running water is a good remedy for mites, spider mites, and thrips, which like seasonal heat and dryness. It is enough to just wet the plants, being careful not to do so at the hottest part of the day. Another use for water is pressure washing the plants to get rid of aphids and other insects that are easy to wash off.

Nettle

It stimulates growth and strengthens the plant's defenses against aphids. Combats mites, chlorosis due to mineral deficiencies, and mildew. Two pounds of fresh plant or three of dried plant in two and a half gallons of water is allowed to ferment for a week. Then dilute twenty times and use it to water the young plants.

If you add horsetail, it is even more effective.

Potash

Potash soap or black soap combat soft-shelled insects such as aphids, mealybugs, and red spider mites, as well as most fungi such as alternaria, botrytis, powdery mildew, or mildew.

Heat 5 quarts of water to 120°F (40°C) and pour into a plastic bucket. Then add two pounds (1 kg) of potassium hydroxide flakes until dissolved, wearing gloves and goggles. Then 5 quarts (5 liters) of used oil is added (kitchen oil is sufficient). Stir for at least one hour and let stand about 15 days.

0.3 ounces (10 g) of this mixture is dissolved in one quart of water to combat whitefly and 0.7 to 1 ounces (20 to 30 grams) in a liter against aphids, mealybugs, and thrips. It can be sprayed on the plant. Potash is effective due to its corrosive power on the chitin of the insects' backs.

It should not be used with hard water, so be careful. It is best to test the mixture before on a few test plants.

Pyrethrum or pyrethrin

Pyrethrum is a natural insecticide extracted from the plant *Chrysanthemum cinerariaefolium*. Dried flowers of the plant are pulverized and mixed with water at a rate of 2 ounces per liter. After 24 hours it can be used. It is toxic to aphids, cabbage flies, whiteflies, mites, fleas, and so on. Be careful, because like rotenone, it is highly toxic to fish.

Rhubarb

Infusions of rhubarb, a common plant in our fields, at 17 ounces (500 grams) per 2.5 gallons (10 liters) of water, will fight black aphids on bean plants.

Horsetail is a potent diuretic in infusion, and also has insecticidal and fungicidal properties against aphids and fungi.

Rotenone

It is an organic insecticide accepted by organic farming. It comes from a plant that grows in the Amazon, the cube or barcasco, grown for this purpose. The indigenous people threw the roots into the river and waited for dead fish to appear, and cooked the roots to extract the poison placed on the tips of their arrows.

Since 1884, the *Lonchocarpus utilitis* and other plant varieties are cultivated to extract the insecticide from the roots. It is effective against whiteflies, aphids, thrips, spider mites, ticks, lice, and fleas, among others, but is also harmful to bees and especially fish, so it should never be dumped in a pond or river.

Seaweed

They bear mentioning, since there is a species called *Lithothamne*, a small calcaric seaweed about an inch long that lives underwater and is not fixed to the ocean floor. In its tiny stem, it crystallizes minerals from the sea water. It is used as a food for humans and a nutritional supplement for the soil, as well as a natural fungicide and insecticide.

We do not recommend the use of a plant that is harvested from the ocean, since its widespread use in agriculture would mean its days are numbered as a species.

Soapy water

This serves to get rid of annoying leaf eaters like aphids, cabbage worms, the ants that accompany aphids, and some fungi, like sooty mold.

It is prepared by diluting 3 to 10 ounces of green soap (like Lagarto) in 2.5 gallons of warm water. Apply it when it is lukewarm, before it gets cold.

Sodium bicarbonate

In addition to helping stomach pain, it is used in the garden to combat anthracnose, blight, mildew, and powdery mildew. It is prepared by mixing a tablespoon with two and a half of vegetable oil, and a half of soap. Apply once a week as long as the infection lasts.

Sugar

This is a good ant trap, since they are irresistibly attracted to honey, condensed milk, or syrup in their path. In reality, it won't get rid of them, but you can entertain yourself by emptying the pots and watching them pour out of the nest.

Sulfur

Sulfur can be used several ways and its effectiveness is directly related to its fineness, purity, and adhesive power. As a preventative measure, it destroys the reproductive structures of fungi, and as a cure, it attacks the mycelium and prevents the growth of the hypha (little roots), which in old fungi interlace so much it prevents the powder from even penetrating them. Wettable sulfur is obtained by mechanical grinding to obtain a very fine powder, with adjuvants added to make it soluble in water.

Tansy

This is another common herb, known as chrysanthemum (*Chrysanthemum vulgare*), whose infusions and decoctions at 10 ounces (300 grams) of fresh grass for two and a half (ten liters) of water will fight all kinds of insects and some worms.

Nettle is hemostatic, astringent, anti-anemic, diuretic, restorative, and is also a good insecticide. We know then that we must not get rid of this plant as enthusiastically as we would other weeds.

Insecticide pellets

It is not a joke. I would not advise anyone to go out and buy a BB gun, but if you happen to have one and **your property has tent caterpillar nests, you can use these pellets invented by the biologist Luis Rejat, pest management technician.** The pellets carry a small dose of insecticide. If only it were ecological!

Tomato

The suckers that you pluck from tomatoes as they grow will serve us not only as fertilizer, but also for making infusions which, after steeping for twelve hours, make a good insecticide against aphids.

White lupin

Lupin beans, salty and sweet, were one of the favorite snacks of moviegoers in other times. They are the seeds of *Lupinus albus*, a plant with blue flowers, and they look like small fava beans. They contain a toxic alkaloid that is eliminated for human consumption when boiled. We want to use raw, chopped beans, though, to extract the oil, and spread on the base of the trees, in order to repel ants.

Wormwood

Take advantage of the leaves and flowers of *Artemisia absinthium*, also known as absinthe, which contain a bitter substance called thujone, which gives absinthe and Pernod their flavor. It can be used by grinding 10 oz of fresh leaves or 1 oz of dry leaves in 1 quart of water for a week. Filter it and spray on every 15 days. This will help control ants, aphids, and caterpillars. As an infusion, it controls mites and slugs, and as a decoction, it fights cabbage worms. To cook, boil 3 oz of dry leaves in a quart of water for 20 minutes, and let sit for a full day. Then dilute it 10 times and sprinkle on plants affected by aphids. Another way to use it is diluting it by 10 and adding classic dish soap. Spray on.

§205.601 Synthetic substances allowed for use in organic crop production.

In accordance with restrictions specified in this section, the following synthetic substances may be used in organic crop production: Provided, that, use of such substances do not contribute to contamination of crops, soil, or water. Substances allowed by this section, except disinfectants and sanitizers in paragraph (a) and those substances in paragraphs (c), (j), (k), and (l) of this section, may only be used when the provisions set forth in §205.206(a) through (d) prove insufficient to prevent or control the target pest.

(a) As algicide, disinfectants, and sanitizer, including irrigation system cleaning systems.
(1) Alcohols.
   (i) Ethanol.
   (ii) Isopropanol.
(2) Chlorine materials—For pre-harvest use, residual chlorine levels in the water in direct crop contact or as water from cleaning irrigation systems applied to soil must not exceed the maximum residual disinfectant limit under the Safe Drinking Water Act, except that chlorine products may be used in edible sprout production according to EPA label directions.
   (i) Calcium hypochlorite.
   (ii) Chlorine dioxide.
   (iii) Sodium hypochlorite.
(3) Copper sulfate—for use as an algicide in aquatic rice systems, is limited to one application per field during any 24-month period. Application rates are limited to those which do not increase baseline soil test values for copper over a timeframe agreed upon by the producer and accredited certifying agent.
(4) Hydrogen peroxide.
(5) Ozone gas—for use as an irrigation system cleaner only.
(6) Peracetic acid—for use in disinfecting equipment, seed, and asexually propagated planting material. Also permitted in hydrogen peroxide formulations as allowed in §205.601(a) at concentration of no more than 6% as indicated on the pesticide product label.
(7) Soap-based algicide/demossers.
(8) Sodium carbonate peroxyhydrate (CAS #-15630-89-4)—Federal law restricts the use of this substance in food crop production to approved food uses identified on the product label.
(b) As herbicides, weed barriers, as applicable.
(1) Herbicides, soap-based—for use in farmstead maintenance (roadways, ditches, right of ways, building perimeters) and ornamental crops.
(2) Mulches.
   (i) Newspaper or other recycled paper, without glossy or colored inks.
   (ii) Plastic mulch and covers (petroleum-based other than polyvinyl chloride (PVC)).
   (iii) Biodegradable biobased mulch film as defined in §205.2. Must be produced without organisms or feedstock derived from excluded methods.
(c) As compost feedstocks—Newspapers or other recycled paper, without glossy or colored inks.

(d) As animal repellents—Soaps, ammonium—for use as a large animal repellant only, no contact with soil or edible portion of crop.
(e) As insecticides (including acaricides or mite control).
(1) Ammonium carbonate—for use as bait in insect traps only, no direct contact with crop or soil.
(2) Aqueous potassium silicate (CAS #-1312-76-1)—the silica, used in the manufacture of potassium silicate, must be sourced from naturally occurring sand.
(3) Boric acid—structural pest control, no direct contact with organic food or crops.
(4) Copper sulfate—for use as tadpole shrimp control in aquatic rice production, is limited to one application per field during any 24-month period. Application rates are limited to levels which do not increase baseline soil test values for copper over a timeframe agreed upon by the producer and accredited certifying agent.
(5) Elemental sulfur.
(6) Lime sulfur—including calcium polysulfide.
(7) Oils, horticultural—narrow range oils as dormant, suffocating, and summer oils.
(8) Soaps, insecticidal.
(9) Sticky traps/barriers.
(10) Sucrose octanoate esters (CAS #s—42922-74-7; 58064-47-4)—in accordance with approved labeling.
(f) As insect management. Pheromones.
(g) As rodenticides. Vitamin D,
(h) As slug or snail bait. Ferric phosphate (CAS # 10045-86-0).
   (i) As plant disease control.
(1) Aqueous potassium silicate (CAS #-1312-76-1)—the silica, used in the manufacture of potassium silicate, must be sourced from naturally occurring sand.
(2) Coppers, fixed—copper hydroxide, copper oxide, copper oxychloride, includes products exempted from EPA tolerance, provided, that, copper-based materials must be used in a manner that minimizes accumulation in the soil and shall not be used as herbicides.
(3) Copper sulfate—Substance must be used in a manner that minimizes accumulation of copper in the soil.
(4) Hydrated lime.
(5) Hydrogen peroxide.
(6) Lime sulfur.
(7) Oils, horticultural, narrow range oils as dormant, suffocating, and summer oils.
(8) Peracetic acid—for use to control fire blight bacteria. Also permitted in hydrogen peroxide formulations as allowed in §205.601(i) at concentration of no more than 6% as indicated on the pesticide product label.
(9) Potassium bicarbonate.
(10) Elemental sulfur.
(11) Streptomycin, for fire blight control in apples and pears only until October 21, 2014.
(12) Tetracycline, for fire blight control in apples and pears only until October 21, 2014.
   (j) As plant or soil amendments.

(1) Aquatic plant extracts (other than hydrolyzed)—Extraction process is limited to the use of potassium hydroxide or sodium hydroxide; solvent amount used is limited to that amount necessary for extraction.

(2) Elemental sulfur.
(3) Humic acids—naturally occurring deposits, water and alkali extracts only.
(4) Lignin sulfonate—chelating agent, dust suppressant.
(5) Magnesium sulfate—allowed with a documented soil deficiency.
(6) Micronutrients—not to be used as a defoliant, herbicide, or desiccant. Those made from nitrates or chlorides are not allowed. Soil deficiency must be documented by testing.
   (i) Soluble boron products.
   (ii) Sulfates, carbonates, oxides, or silicates of zinc, copper, iron, manganese, molybdenum, selenium, and cobalt.
(7) Liquid fish products—can be pH adjusted with sulfuric, citric or phosphoric acid. The amount of acid used shall not exceed the minimum needed to lower the pH to 3.5.
(8) Vitamins, B_1, C, and E.
(9) Sulfurous acid (CAS # 7782-99-2) for on-farm generation of substance utilizing 99% purity elemental sulfur per paragraph (j)(2) of this section.
   (k) As plant growth regulators. Ethylene gas—for regulation of pineapple flowering.
   (l) As floating agents in postharvest handling.
(1) Lignin sulfonate.
(2) Sodium silicate—for tree fruit and fiber processing.
   (m) As synthetic inert ingredients as classified by the Environmental Protection Agency (EPA), for use with nonsynthetic substances or synthetic substances listed in this section and used as an active pesticide ingredient in accordance with any limitations on the use of such substances.
(1) EPA List 4—Inerts of Minimal Concern.
(2) EPA List 3—Inerts of unknown toxicity—for use only in passive pheromone dispensers.
   (n) Seed preparations. Hydrogen chloride (CAS # 7647-01-0)—for delinting cotton seed for planting.
   (o) As production aids. Microcrystalline cheesewax (CAS #'s 64742-42-3, 8009-03-08, and 8002-74-2)-for use in log grown mushroom production. Must be made without either ethylene-propylene co-polymer or synthetic colors.

§205.602 Nonsynthetic substances prohibited for use in organic crop production.

The following nonsynthetic substances may not be used in organic crop production:

(a) Ash from manure burning.
(b) Arsenic.
(c) Calcium chloride, brine process is natural and prohibited for use except as a foliar spray to treat a physiological disorder associated with calcium uptake.
(d) Lead salts.
(e) Potassium chloride—unless derived from a mined source and applied in a manner that minimizes chloride accumulation in the soil.
(f) Sodium fluoaluminate (mined).

(g) Sodium nitrate—unless use is restricted to no more than 20% of the crop's total nitrogen requirement; use in spirulina production is unrestricted until October 21, 2005.

(h) Strychnine.

(i) Tobacco dust (nicotine sulfate).

§205.603 Synthetic substances allowed for use in organic livestock production.

In accordance with restrictions specified in this section the following synthetic substances may be used in organic livestock production:

(a) As disinfectants, sanitizer, and medical treatments as applicable.

(1) Alcohols.

  (i) Ethanol-disinfectant and sanitizer only, prohibited as a feed additive.

  (ii) Isopropanol-disinfectant only.

(2) Aspirin-approved for health care use to reduce inflammation.

(3) Atropine (CAS #-51-55-8)—federal law restricts this drug to use by or on the lawful written or oral order of a licensed veterinarian, in full compliance with the AMDUCA and 21 CFR part 530 of the Food and Drug Administration regulations. Also, for use under 7 CFR part 205, the NOP requires:

  (i) Use by or on the lawful written order of a licensed veterinarian; and

  (ii) A meat withdrawal period of at least 56 days after administering to livestock intended for slaughter; and a milk discard period of at least 12 days after administering to dairy animals.

(4) Biologics—Vaccines.

(5) Butorphanol (CAS #-42408-82-2)—federal law restricts this drug to use by or on the lawful written or oral order of a licensed veterinarian, in full compliance with the AMDUCA and 21 CFR part 530 of the Food and Drug Administration regulations. Also, for use under 7 CFR part 205, the NOP requires:

  (i) Use by or on the lawful written order of a licensed veterinarian; and

  (ii) A meat withdrawal period of at least 42 days after administering to livestock intended for slaughter; and a milk discard period of at least 8 days after administering to dairy animals.

(6) Chlorhexidine—Allowed for surgical procedures conducted by a veterinarian. Allowed for use as a teat dip when alternative germicidal agents and/or physical barriers have lost their effectiveness.

(7) Chlorine materials—disinfecting and sanitizing facilities and equipment. Residual chlorine levels in the water shall not exceed the maximum residual disinfectant limit under the Safe Drinking Water Act.

  (i) Calcium hypochlorite.

  (ii) Chlorine dioxide.

  (iii) Sodium hypochlorite.

(8) Electrolytes—without antibiotics.

(9) Flunixin (CAS #-38677-85-9)—in accordance with approved labeling; except that for use under 7 CFR part 205, the NOP requires a withdrawal period of at least two-times that required by the FDA.

(10) Furosemide (CAS #-54-31-9)—in accordance with approved labeling; except that for use under 7 CFR part 205, the NOP requires a withdrawal period of at least two-times that required that required by the FDA.

(11) Glucose.

(12) Glycerin—Allowed as a livestock teat dip, must be produced through the hydrolysis of fats or oils.

(13) Hydrogen peroxide.

(14) Iodine.

(15) Magnesium hydroxide (CAS #-1309-42-8)—federal law restricts this drug to use by or on the lawful written or oral order of a licensed veterinarian, in full compliance with the AMDUCA and 21 CFR part 530 of the Food and Drug Administration regulations. Also, for use under 7 CFR part 205, the NOP requires use by or on the lawful written order of a licensed veterinarian.

(16) Magnesium sulfate.

(17) Oxytocin—use in postparturition therapeutic applications.

(18) Parasiticides—Prohibited in slaughter stock, allowed in emergency treatment for dairy and breeder stock when organic system plan-approved preventive management does not prevent infestation. Milk or milk products from a treated animal cannot be labeled as provided for in subpart D of this part for 90 days following treatment. In breeder stock, treatment cannot occur during the last third of gestation if the progeny will be sold as organic and must not be used during the lactation period for breeding stock.

  (i) Fenbendazole (CAS #43210-67-9)—only for use by or on the lawful written order of a licensed veterinarian.

  (ii) Ivermectin (CAS #70288-86-7).

  (iii) Moxidectin (CAS #113507-06-5)—for control of internal parasites only.

(19) Peroxyacetic/peracetic acid (CAS #-79-21-0)—for sanitizing facility and processing equipment.

(20) Phosphoric acid—allowed as an equipment cleaner, *provided*, that, no direct contact with organically managed livestock or land occurs.

(21) Poloxalene (CAS #-9003-11-6)—for use under 7 CFR part 205, the NOP requires that poloxalene only be used for the emergency treatment of bloat.

(22) Tolazoline (CAS #-59-98-3)—federal law restricts this drug to use by or on the lawful written or oral order of a licensed veterinarian, in full compliance with the AMDUCA and 21 CFR part 530 of the Food and Drug Administration regulations. Also, for use under 7 CFR part 205, the NOP requires:

  (i) Use by or on the lawful written order of a licensed veterinarian;

  (ii) Use only to reverse the effects of sedation and analgesia caused by Xylazine; and

  (iii) A meat withdrawal period of at least 8 days after administering to livestock intended for slaughter; and a milk discard period of at least 4 days after administering to dairy animals.

(23) Xylazine (CAS #-7361-61-7)—federal law restricts this drug to use by or on the lawful written or oral order of a licensed veterinarian, in full compliance with the AMDUCA and 21 CFR part 530 of the Food and Drug Administration regulations. Also, for use under 7 CFR part 205, the NOP requires:

  (i) Use by or on the lawful written order of a licensed veterinarian;

  (ii) The existence of an emergency; and

  (iii) A meat withdrawal period of at least 8 days after administering to livestock intended for slaughter; and a milk discard period of at least 4 days after administering to dairy animals.

(b) As topical treatment, external parasiticide or local anesthetic as applicable.

(1) Copper sulfate.

(2) Formic acid (CAS # 64-18-6)—for use as a pesticide solely within honeybee hives.

(3) Iodine.

(4) Lidocaine—as a local anesthetic. Use requires a withdrawal period of 90 days after administering to livestock intended for slaughter and 7 days after administering to dairy animals.

(5) Lime, hydrated—as an external pest control, not permitted to cauterize physical alterations or deodorize animal wastes.

(6) Mineral oil—for topical use and as a lubricant.

(7) Procaine—as a local anesthetic, use requires a withdrawal period of 90 days after administering to livestock intended for slaughter and 7 days after administering to dairy animals.

(8) Sucrose octanoate esters (CAS #s-42922-74-7; 58064-47-4)—in accordance with approved labeling.

(c) As feed supplements—None.

(d) As feed additives.

(1) DL-Methionine, DL-Methionine-hydroxy analog, and DL-Methionine-hydroxy analog calcium (CAS #'s 59-51-8, 583-91-5, 4857-44-7, and 922-50-9)—for use only in organic poultry production at the following maximum levels of synthetic methionine per ton of feed: Laying and broiler chickens—2 pounds; turkeys and all other poultry—3 pounds.

(2) Trace minerals, used for enrichment or fortification when FDA approved.

(3) Vitamins, used for enrichment or fortification when FDA approved.

(e) As synthetic inert ingredients as classified by the Environmental Protection Agency (EPA), for use with nonsynthetic substances or synthetic substances listed in this section and used as an active pesticide ingredient in accordance with any limitations on the use of such substances.

(1) EPA List 4—Inerts of Minimal Concern.

(f) Excipients, only for use in the manufacture of drugs used to treat organic livestock when the excipient is: Identified by the FDA as Generally Recognized As Safe; Approved by the FDA as a food additive; or Included in the FDA review and approval of a New Animal Drug Application or New Drug Application.

§205.604 Nonsynthetic substances prohibited for use in organic livestock production.

The following nonsynthetic substances may not be used in organic livestock production:

(a) Strychnine.

§205.605 Nonagricultural (nonorganic) substances allowed as ingredients in or on processed products labeled as "organic" or "made with organic (specified ingredients or food group(s))."

The following nonagricultural substances may be used as ingredients in or on processed products labeled as "organic" or "made with organic (specified ingredients or food group(s))" only in accordance with any restrictions specified in this section.

(a) *Nonsynthetics allowed:*

Acids (Alginic; Citric—produced by microbial fermentation of carbohydrate substances; and Lactic).

Agar-agar.

Animal enzymes—(Rennet—animals derived; Catalase—bovine liver; Animal lipase; Pancreatin; Pepsin; and Trypsin).

Attapulgite—as a processing aid in the handling of plant and animal oils.

Bentonite.

Calcium carbonate.

Calcium chloride.
Calcium sulfate—mined.
Carrageenan.
Dairy cultures.
Diatomaceous earth—food filtering aid only.
Egg white lysozyme (CAS # 9001-63-2)
Enzymes—must be derived from edible, nontoxic plants, nonpathogenic fungi, or nonpathogenic bacteria.
Flavors, nonsynthetic sources only and must not be produced using synthetic solvents and carrier systems or any artificial preservative.
Gellan gum (CAS # 71010-52-1)—high-acyl form only.
Glucono delta-lactone—production by the oxidation of D-glucose with bromine water is prohibited.
Kaolin.
L-Malic acid (CAS # 97-67-6).
Magnesium sulfate, nonsynthetic sources only.
Microorganisms—any food grade bacteria, fungi, and other microorganism.
Nitrogen—oil-free grades.
Oxygen—oil-free grades.
Perlite—for use only as a filter aid in food processing.
Potassium chloride.
Potassium iodide.
Sodium bicarbonate.
Sodium carbonate.
Tartaric acid—made from grape wine.
Waxes—nonsynthetic (Carnauba wax; and Wood resin).
Yeast—When used as food or a fermentation agent in products labeled as "organic," yeast must be organic if its end use is for human consumption; nonorganic yeast may be used when organic yeast is not commercially available. Growth on petrochemical substrate and sulfite waste liquor is prohibited. For smoked yeast, nonsynthetic smoke flavoring process must be documented.

(b) *Synthetics allowed:*
Acidified sodium chlorite—Secondary direct antimicrobial food treatment and indirect food contact surface sanitizing. Acidified with citric acid only.
Activated charcoal (CAS #s 7440-44-0; 64365-11-3)—only from vegetative sources; for use only as a filtering aid.
Alginates.
Ammonium bicarbonate—for use only as a leavening agent.
Ammonium carbonate—for use only as a leavening agent.
Ascorbic acid.
Calcium citrate.
Calcium hydroxide.
Calcium phosphates (monobasic, dibasic, and tribasic).
Carbon dioxide.
Cellulose—for use in regenerative casings, as an anti-caking agent (non-chlorine bleached) and filtering aid.
Chlorine materials—disinfecting and sanitizing food contact surfaces, *except,* that, residual chlorine levels in the water shall not exceed the maximum residual disinfectant limit under the Safe Drinking Water Act (Calcium hypochlorite; Chlorine dioxide; and Sodium hypochlorite).
Cyclohexylamine (CAS # 108-91-8)—for use only as a boiler water additive for packaging sterilization.
Diethylaminoethanol (CAS # 100-37-8)—for use only as a boiler water additive for packaging sterilization.
Ethylene—allowed for postharvest ripening of tropical fruit and degreening of citrus.
Ferrous sulfate—for iron enrichment or

fortification of foods when required by regulation or recommended (independent organization).
Glycerides (mono and di)—for use only in drum drying of food.
Glycerin—produced by hydrolysis of fats and oils.
Hydrogen peroxide.
Magnesium carbonate—for use only in agricultural products labeled "made with organic (specified ingredients or food group(s))," prohibited in agricultural products labeled "organic".
Magnesium chloride—derived from sea water.
Magnesium stearate—for use only in agricultural products labeled "made with organic (specified ingredients or food group(s))," prohibited in agricultural products labeled "organic".
Nutrient vitamins and minerals, in accordance with 21 CFR 104.20, Nutritional Quality Guidelines For Foods.
Octadecylamine (CAS # 124-30-1)—for use only as a boiler water additive for packaging sterilization.
Ozone.
Peracetic acid/Peroxyacetic acid (CAS # 79-21-0)—for use in wash and/or rinse water according to FDA limitations. For use as a sanitizer on food contact surfaces.
Phosphoric acid—cleaning of food-contact surfaces and equipment only.
Potassium acid tartrate.
Potassium carbonate.
Potassium citrate.
Potassium hydroxide—prohibited for use in lye peeling of fruits and vegetables except when used for peeling peaches.
Potassium phosphate—for use only in agricultural products labeled "made with organic (specific ingredients or food group(s))," prohibited in agricultural products labeled "organic".
Silicon dioxide—Permitted as a defoamer. Allowed for other uses when organic rice hulls are not commercially available.
Sodium acid pyrophosphate (CAS # 7758-16-9)—for use only as a leavening agent.
Sodium citrate.
Sodium hydroxide—prohibited for use in lye peeling of fruits and vegetables.
Sodium phosphates—for use only in dairy foods.
Sulfur dioxide—for use only in wine labeled "made with organic grapes," Provided, That, total sulfite concentration does not exceed 100 ppm.
Tetrasodium pyrophosphate (CAS # 7722-88-5)—for use only in meat analog products.
Tocopherols—derived from vegetable oil when rosemary extracts are not a suitable alternative.
Xanthan gum.

§205.606 Nonorganically produced agricultural products allowed as ingredients in or on processed products labeled as "organic."

Only the following nonorganically produced agricultural products may be used as ingredients in or on processed products labeled as "organic," only in accordance with any restrictions specified in this section, and only when the product is not commercially available in organic form.
(a) Casings, from processed intestines.
(b) Celery powder.
(c) Chia (*Salvia hispanica L.*).
(d) Colors derived from agricultural products—Must not be produced using synthetic solvents and carrier systems or any artificial preservative.

(1) Beet juice extract color (pigment CAS #7659-95-2).
(2) Beta-carotene extract color—derived from carrots or algae (pigment CAS# 7235-40-7).
(3) Black currant juice color (pigment CAS #'s: 528-58-5, 528-53-0, 643-84-5, 134-01-0, 1429-30-7, and 134-04-3).
(4) Black/Purple carrot juice color (pigment CAS #'s: 528-58-5, 528-53-0, 643-84-5, 134-01-0, 1429-30-7, and 134-04-3).
(5) Blueberry juice color (pigment CAS #'s: 528-58-5, 528-53-0, 643-84-5, 134-01-0, 1429-30-7, and 134-04-3).
(6) Carrot juice color (pigment CAS #1393-63-1).
(7) Cherry juice color (pigment CAS #'s: 528-58-5, 528-53-0, 643-84-5, 134-01-0, 1429-30-7, and 134-04-3).
(8) Chokeberry—Aronia juice color (pigment CAS #'s: 528-58-5, 528-53-0, 643-84-5, 134-01-0, 1429-30-7, and 134-04-3).
(9) Elderberry juice color (pigment CAS #'s: 528-58-5, 528-53-0, 643-84-5, 134-01-0, 1429-30-7, and 134-04-3).
(10) Grape juice color (pigment CAS #'s: 528-58-5, 528-53-0, 643-84-5, 134-01-0, 1429-30-7, and 134-04-3).
(11) Grape skin extract color (pigment CAS #'s: 528-58-5, 528-53-0, 643-84-5, 134-01-0, 1429-30-7, and 134-04-3).
(12) Paprika color (CAS #68917-78-2)—dried, and oil extracted.
(13) Pumpkin juice color (pigment CAS #127-40-2).
(14) Purple potato juice (pigment CAS #'s: 528-58-5, 528-53-0, 643-84-5, 134-01-0, 1429-30-7, and 134-04-3).
(15) Red cabbage extract color (pigment CAS #'s: 528-58-5, 528-53-0, 643-84-5, 134-01-0, 1429-30-7, and 134-04-3).
(16) Red radish extract color (pigment CAS #'s: 528-58-5, 528-53-0, 643-84-5, 134-01-0, 1429-30-7, and 134-04-3).
(17) Saffron extract color (pigment CAS #1393-63-1).
(18) Turmeric extract color (CAS #458-37-7).
(e) Dillweed oil (CAS # 8006-75-5).
(f) Fish oil (Fatty acid CAS #'s: 10417-94-4, and 25167-62-8)—stabilized with organic ingredients or only with ingredients on the National List, §§205.605 and 205.606.
(g) Fortified cooking wines.
(1) Marsala.
(2) Sherry.
(h) Fructooligosaccharides (CAS # 308066-66-2).
(i) Galangal, frozen.
(j) Gelatin (CAS # 9000-70-8).
(k) Gums—water extracted only (Arabic; Guar; Locust bean; and Carob bean).
(l) Inulin-oligofructose enriched (CAS # 9005-80-5).
(m) Kelp—for use only as a thickener and dietary supplement.
(n) Konjac flour (CAS # 37220-17-0).
(o) Lecithin—de-oiled.
(p) Lemongrass—frozen.
(q) Orange pulp, dried.
(r) Orange shellac-unbleached (CAS # 9000-59-3).
(s) Pectin (non-amidated forms only).
(t) Peppers (Chipotle chile).
(u) Seaweed, Pacific kombu.
(v) Starches.
(1) Cornstarch (native).
(2) Sweet potato starch—for bean thread production only.
(w) Tragacanth gum (CAS #-9000-65-1).
(x) Turkish bay leaves.
(y) Wakame seaweed (*Undaria pinnatifida*).
(z) Whey protein concentrate.

Gardening in the home

What we should know about
balcony gardens

Having a terrace is a privilege because it enables us to eat well for several weeks out of the year.

At the moment of truth, you may have no more space than a balcony or terrace for a small home garden. No problem. Look at all the things you can do or fit in a small space:

● A small compost where your organic kitchen waste and scraps from the garden are transformed into compost. The vermicomposters are relatively small, and the worms prevent bad odors.

● A container for growing potatoes. In this case, biodynamic farming recommends stacking several tires, but a can takes up less space and one plant can produce more than twenty potatoes.

● Hang baskets on your balcony to make seedbeds or grow herbs. If you have a terrace you can try to make a grid or wooden lattice to cover the top like a trellis.

● On the lattice that you place on the walls and columns you can grow vines and make vine arbors with any climbing plant, like cucumbers.

● Place the pots in tiers for better use of light and you can have tomatoes, peppers, and eggplants within a short distance of each other.

● Even easier is to buy bags of potting soil and, without tearing them, simply make a hole and sow beans, tomatoes, or peppers.

● Use all containers you have on hand for the garden: an old aquarium, cut drums, and even a bathtub can be useful if you don't want to buy pots.

● Sow germinated seeds in the windowsills.

● Build a corner for aromatic plants.

● Collect rainwater from the roof in a fifty-gallon drum, the kind that are discarded in the chemical industries. You can ask for one; they'll probably give it to you for free.

● Plant species of dwarf fruit trees that produce berries or fruit.

With a few simple drawers, we can build a compost bin on the terrace. Just have a space for new waste and another for the decomposition to occur for several weeks.

The garden on the balcony

Potted plants

The list of plants that can be grown in pots is great. Here's an example: chard, eggplant, zucchini, onions, spinach, beans, lettuce, potatoes, peppers, leeks, cabbage, tomatoes, and carrots. You have to take care of them better than if they were in the ground, getting pots or containers that are 12 to 20 inches deep (the 20 for zucchini and carrots) and watering more often, because if the sun touches them, the pots dry out quickly .

If your balcony is on a low floor and has no more than four hours of sun, you can only grow plants that do not need much light. Forget tomatoes or choose smaller species that are more resistant to lack of light. Sow primarily lettuce and spinach. Parsley also grows well in the shade.

Occasionally, turn the pots, so they do not always grow in the same direction. Try to get seeds of dwarf varieties of tomatoes, cabbage, or lettuce. Do not leave spaces uncultivated, and be always ready with seedlings to transplant a plant when you remove another.

The design of the balcony

Since we will have a very limited space, we have to extract maximum performance: the floor, walls, and ceiling should be utilized fully. Put in shelves, racks, wall planters, and lattices for climbing plants, and also dwarf fruit trees and tiered pots.

Tomatoes planted in pots will soon need a support. Try not to leave more than one or two plants in each of the pots.

The light and the sun

A terrace is not the same as a balcony, nor is living in a wet climate the same as a dry one. In southern Spain, the terraces in summer tend to be uninhabited, but that gives us the possibility to build a lattice with poles that will provide a lovely shade and allow us to have climbing plants, like vining beans, zucchini, or chayote vines.

Soil and water

Having a garden at home involves at least the same obligations as having a plot. The soil must be well fertilized. A mixture of sand or normal soil with 50 percent compost and a layer of gravel at the bottom will work well.

In watering is where you will find more differences, since here the much needed drainage passes through the soil, and more than ever we need to consider drip irrigation. In such a small space it will be easy to set up, and necessary if you plan to go on vacation in the summer. There are other economic tricks, of course. You can purchase water-filled plastic bottles attached to the planters with a narrow tube that makes a siphon, so that they will

Fruit trees in pots

Lemon, orange, pomegranate, persimmon, cherry, pear, apple, quince, plum, currant, and raspberry plants can be grown in pots. **If you want an orange tree in your garden, you can choose between Bunge, Bouquet, and Navelina varieties, but only the latter will offer sweet and edible fruits**. When you choose a fruit for your balcony, pay attention to the species, as most are ornamental and fruits are bitter. Caring for them is very easy. Just get a flower pot and fill it with nutrient-rich soil, like a well-worked garden. In winter to help the fruit stay on the tree, it is best to help the tree with a dose of nutrients including iron, magnesium, zinc, and potassium. **Water it well and wet the leaves in hot weather; prune the shoots in spring to avoid losing the shape and protect it from frost**. The orange tree is best brought indoors if you live in cold areas. Remember that in Seville they are planted in the streets, but in Paris they are stored in warehouses.

The layout of the garden according to your needs

Each master has his own booklet, according to one proverb. That booklet is experience, so do not hesitate to experiment until you get the best result.

When gardening, it is most common to make straight furrows to facilitate planting and installing stakes in the case of climbing plants. If the ground is slightly sloped, contour lines can be used to keep furrows as horizontal as possible, so that irrigation and rainwater are maximized.

Biodynamic farming suggests that ridges should be oriented north to south along the energy lines, but if the garden is on a hillside you must adapt to the contours. Sometimes there is no choice so an orchard with rows oriented from east to west should work just fine. There will always be plants with more sunlight exposure than others.

Planting in circles

Some experienced gardeners have decided to implement other methods of planting. For example, planting in circles: they begin making a circular ridge, then sowing in the center, and mulching right after. The idea is to compare this type of planting with a linear planting located right next to it and, from this point on, experiment in every possible way. The classic furrows—15 to 20 inches apart, 8" to 12" high, and 15" to 20" wide—can be replaced by circles, spirals, or serpentines, depending on the possibilities of the garden.

When planning the layout of the garden, you must take into account that some plants need more sun than others..

The classical system

In a traditional garden there is a path down the center, which can be paved, and crosses the property, preferably from east to west. Alongside the path, the rectangular beds are in place.

If the weather is dry, furrows and ridges should be of equal width; thus, the gardener creates a jungle in which the plants themselves retain moisture, preventing the sun from reaching the ground. Nevertheless, this has its risks, because if it rains too much, pests and diseases caused by excess moisture could strike. It can also hinder harvest if the beds are too large.

If the weather is wet, furrows are narrow and ridges are wide, thus letting light and air circulate. If the foliage is abundant, it also allows you to walk through the plants. So say the ridge is 3 feet (1 m) wide and the furrow 1.5 feet (50 cm). The plant is rooted half in the wet area and half in the wide ridge's dry zone. With this system, which requires more space, you facilitate harvesting and maintenance work.

Some gardeners prefer very wide furrows and narrow ridges, so irrigation holds more water. This implies that the soil will

If you have trees, make sure that the shadow does not affect the garden, and watch the distance, as some, such as poplar, are harmful to the garden.

Plan carefully the areas you will tread when working in the garden. Sometimes tomato plants are too close together and the precious fruit cannot be reached without damaging plants.

In the image, the three models of furrows that can be used in the home garden. The first two need plenty of space. **Upper left**: circles. **Right**: spiral. They require planning to take advantage of positive associations between plants. **Lower image**: the traditional way.

dry faster and will crack when the sun hits it. Also, you would have to step in the mud to get in between plants.

Tubers, such as the potato, are planted in rows at equal distances; you will not have to get in between, except for removing beetles and weeding. To the contrary, tomatoes and beans involve many trips up and down to clean and harvest. Cabbage, lettuce, onions, and carrots are usually planted close together to maximize the field, because all you need to do between the rows is harvest. They can also be potted without furrows. Garlic, lima beans, peas, string beans, peppers, and eggplant do not offer major trouble to walk through, but it is better if the ridges are not too narrow. Pumpkins, squash, and cucumbers have no problems, because they are always planted apart and can invade their surrounding area for several feet.

The spiral garden

This method has been developed in the field of bio-horticulture. It involves significant initial work but it is reduced in subsequent years.

The cultivation is done on an elevation that has the form of an elongated hill. It is best to mark the spiral on the ground at the beginning. You start to dig a ridge from the outside: 5 ft. (1.5 meters) wide and 20 inches (50 cm) in height. You do this using a big hoe, throwing the soil as loose as possible in the center.

Turn inward progressively to end up in the center of the spiral. As you turn, leave a separation of 32 inches between "ridges" in order to be able to delve into the unique ridge of the garden. Then everything is mulched with straw and only uncovered for planting.

Apparently, this system prevents diseases and maintains good availability of land, spreading positive energy throughout the garden. If you choose this system ensure that the plants do not block the light to each other.

Rotation

It is practiced because of different nutritional needs in the garden. For example, not many plants that need a lot of nutrients are supposed to be planted right after the other; beets will not be planted after cabbages.

Here is a list of plants that need more fertilizer: chard, celery, squash, zucchini, cabbage, spinach, lettuce, corn, cucumbers, leeks, and potatoes. Try not to repeat any of these plants in the same area.

Now look at the plants that are less demanding and can follow the above, provided that the ground is fertilized again: garlic, onions, some lettuce, endive, turnips, beets, and carrots.

And finally, plants that do not only need little fertilizer but also enrich the soil: all legumes, peas, beans, lentils, and chickpeas.

Do not plant vegetables of the same species in the same place two years in a row, like cabbages and cauliflowers. Also do not cultivate plants of the same family like cruciferous vegetables (radishes and turnips), umbelliferae (celery and carrot), or cucurbits (pumpkins and squash). The classic four-year rotation divides the garden into four parts. Look at the box below, which contains two examples. Keep in mind that cabbages can grow after legumes in the same year.

Rotation of crops

● **Tall plants**
First year: beans or peas.
Second year: pumpkins, squash, or cucumbers.
Third year: tomatoes.
Fourth year: corn.

● **Short plants**
First year: cabbage or cauliflower, and radishes.
Second year: carrots, turnips, and celery.
Third year: beets or onions.
Fourth year: peppers, eggplants, and potatoes.

Exceptions to the annual rotation

Tomatoes can be planted several years in the same place, leaving the plants on the ground and burying them to serve as fertilizer. **You may use the same place twice in the same year, for example, to plant lettuce—in spring— and turnips in winter. Follow the criteria of rotation.**
Some plants, like strawberries and turnips, stay several years in the same place. If you have room, reserve some time in the four-year rotation to plant cover crops.

Convenient associations in the garden

Keep in mind when rotating, which plants can be associated with one another and which are incompatible. In the next chapter we will discuss this issue further, but regarding rotation and what plants we can plant together in the square of the garden, here are some convenient associations:

● Garlic, carrot, and onion. Some gardeners also add tomato, because the garlic fights mildew.

● Cabbages, lettuce, cucumbers, beans, leeks, and tomatoes.

● Pumpkins, onions, beans, and peas.

● Pumpkins, spinach, carrots, and onions.

● Eggplants and beans fight potato beetles, onions and leeks repel carrot flies, rosemary and thyme repel cabbage flies, basil repels aphids, and generally aromatic plants are friends with the beneficial insects and enemies of harmful ones. However, you better look at the big chart that we offer on pages 136-137 to study possible associations.

Preparing the layout of the garden

Plan it

● **Divide the work plans for the garden into months and seasons.**

● **Write down the dates for sowing and harvesting vegetables,** using the chart.

● **Divide the space between all species**, taking into account the use you will make of them. **Do not plant too many tomatoes if you do not plan on canning** or giving them away.

There are combinations of favorable and unfavorable plants and every gardener should consider them in order to avoid unexpected problems.

Based on the principle of competition, we combine plants with different root and leaf systems: roots at different depths and leaves that do not compete for light. Also, keep in mind that harvest times are different and that nutritional needs are different. There are associations of plants and insects that need each other. There are also plants with certain fungi that live in the roots and make the nitrogen become assimilable for them, like legumes. Throughout the book and in each plant's description we will mention the rivals and friends, which can be good or bad. For example, chillies planted near tomatoes will give them a particular spicy flavor that some people might like but for most it is not advisable.

Some authors have made their own divisions and classifications. For example,

Marianne Hilgers, author of the book *Curso de agricultura ecológica (Organic Farming Course)*, believes that there are four types of associations in the garden:

● **Commensalistic polyculture**, in which one species takes advantage of the other, and the latter does not benefit.
● **Ammensalistic polyculture**, in which one plant is harmed and the other does not feel or suffer, like annuals and perennials interspersed.
● **Monopolistic polyculture**, in which one species benefits and the other is harmed.
● **Inhibitory polyculture**, in which both species are harmed, like when planting sugarcane in a garden interspersed with other plants.

Favorable associations

The main ones are between grasses and legumes, alternating grains, such as barley or rye, with legumes such as alfalfa or clover. This system is used by many farmers that usually plant a legume every two years to recover the lost nitrogen from the soil. However, planting can also be done simultaneously.

The most beneficial association in this sense is the one between corn (a grain) and beans. When the corn reaches a certain height it serves to support beans—planted when they are eight inches (20 cm) tall—and the latter intertwines with the stalk to grow up.

Animals that can help

It is worth remembering that there are many animals that can help us to have an organic garden and to be in communion with nature. So do not be afraid of frogs, as a single one can eat more than ten thousand harmful insects every three months—including crickets, bedbugs, and harmful caterpillars—while at the same time it respects the earthworms that you lovingly care for. Also, we should respect insectivorous birds, such as swallows, and attract bats, which fly over the orchard fields, getting rid of annoying pests.

Plants that complement each other

- Eggplants and beans fight potato beetles.
- Onions and leeks combat carrot flies. Plant these with tomatoes (onions should be planted first next to the furrow laid down for tomatoes). Also plant them with radishes and strawberries.
- Garlic combats mildew in tomatoes.
- Parsnips and endive get along in alternation.
- Legumes get along with cabbages and carrots in alternate rows, but not with onions and garlic.

Sowing seasons vary depending on climate. Refer to seed packets for specific details.

Six zones for rotation

- In order to maintain soil quality **you should change crops each year.**
- **Divide** the garden into six parts.
- Three of them should be equal for the rotational crops.
- A fourth part will be assigned to perennial crops such as **artichokes, herbs, or small fruits (raspberries, strawberries, or blueberries)**, depending on the climate.
- A fifth part will be meant for crops that occupy a lot of land, such as pumpkins, melons, or cucumbers.
- A sixth one will be to make compost. It may be smaller and it will accumulate organic remains of plants after their growth cycle is finished.
- **Likewise you will need an area to store tools**, hoes, rakes, shovels, watering cans, hoses, and even better if you can cover it so you can prepare the starter pots. Above all, make sure you plan it.

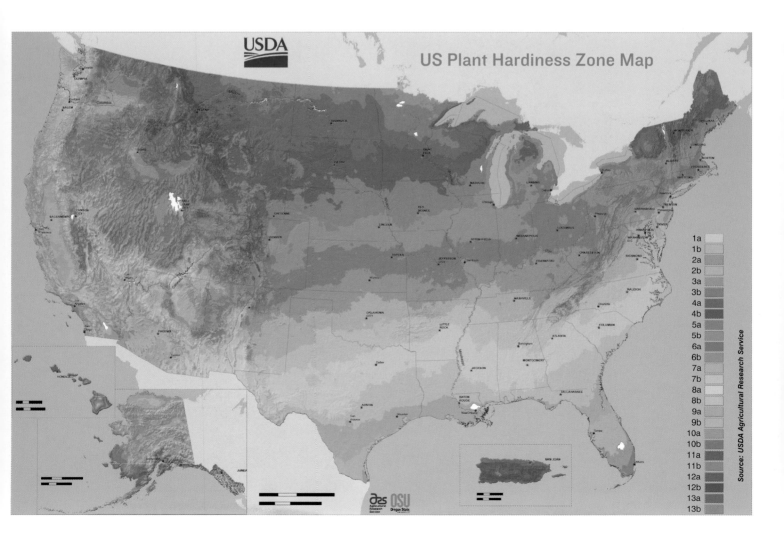

US Plant Hardiness Zone Map

| 1a |
| 1b |
| 2a |
| 2b |
| 3a |
| 3b |
| 4a |
| 4b |
| 5a |
| 5b |
| 6a |
| 6b |
| 7a |
| 7b |
| 8a |
| 8b |
| 9a |
| 9b |
| 10a |
| 10b |
| 11a |
| 11b |
| 12a |
| 12b |
| 13a |
| 13b |

Source: USDA Agricultural Research Service

Association between crops

The data included in this chart is based on experience. Other charts, such as the one from *The Vegetable Gardener's Bible*, suggest different associations—for example, cucumber and tomato are considered friends, whereas potato and tomato adversaries; or cabbage and onions are considered friends while tomatoes and corn enemies—thus contradicting the chart presented below, which indicates that there is no general and absolute law for such relationships.

	Beneficial association	Unfavorable association
chard	celery, lettuce, onions	asparagus, leeks, tomatoes
chicory	lettuce, fennel, tomatoes, onions	cabbage
garlic	strawberries, carrots, turnips, lettuce, peas, beets, potatoes	beans, cabbage, peas
artichoke	lettuce, beans, peas, radish	
celery	lettuce, cabbage, leeks, radish, spinach, tomatoes, cucumbers, beets, beans, chard, peas	corn, parsley, lettuce
eggplants	Beans	potatoes
pumpkin and squash	corn, potatoes, basil, onion, peas, beans	radishes
onions	beets, cucumbers, lettuce, parsley, tomatoes, carrots, strawberries, leeks, spinach, squash, cabbage	cabbage, peas, potatoes, beans
cabbage	beets, beans, lettuce, potatoes, tomatoes, celery, lettuce, peas, cucumbers, leeks	garlic, fennel, chicory, radishes, strawberries, leeks
endive	strawberries, turnip	
asparagus	lettuce, radishes, cucumbers, leeks, tomatoes, parsley, peas	onions, beets
spinach	carrots, onions, turnips, radishes, potatoes, cabbage, beans, strawberries	chard, beets
strawberries	garlic, spinach, lettuce, onions, leek, thyme	cabbage
green peas	asparagus, celery, cabbage, lettuce, turnips, radishes, potatoes, corn, cucumber, carrots	garlic, onions, parsley, leeks
fennel	cabbage, leeks, onions, strawberries, cucumbers, chicory, lettuce, peas	cabbage, tomatoes, beans
beans	eggplant, celery, spinach, lettuce, turnips, radishes, carrots, cabbage, strawberries, corn, potatoes	garlic, fennel, chard, beets, onions
lettuce	beets, chervil, cucumbers, strawberries, onions, peas, carrots, cabbage, lima beans, turnips, leeks, radishes	parsley
corn	cucumbers, peas, beans, tomatoes	beets, potatoes, celery

Indigenous Wisdom

In Central America, subsistence agriculture has always enabled corn, beans, and pumpkins to be planted in the same space. The soil is barely dug on the slopes and the remains of the previous harvest are used as fertilizers. A favorable climate and soil, especially in volcanic areas, allow corn to grow over 13 feet (4 m) and beans thrive between the tall stalks, leaving the ground to the sprawling pumpkins. They are part of a diet that is rich enough to maintain the population.

	Beneficial association	Unfavorable association
turnips	peas, beans, spinach, lettuce, tomato, cucumber, cabbage, leek	
potatoes	garlic, cabbage, beans, peas, tomatoes, celery, lima beans, radishes	eggplant, onions, corn, cucumber, spinach
cucumbers	asparagus, celery, chives, lettuce, peas, basil, cabbage, beans, corn, fennel	potatoes, tomatoes, radishes, beets, parsley, cabbage
leeks	asparagus, spinach, celery, strawberries, onions, carrots, fennel, lettuce, tomatoes	chard, peas, cabbage, pumpkins
radishes	carrots, spinach, lettuce, tomatoes, chervil, beans, peas, garlic, cucumber, leek	
beets	celery, lettuce, onions, cabbage	asparagus, beans, leeks, tomatoes, carrots
tomatoes	garlic, basil, celery, onions, leeks, corn, asparagus, carrots, cabbage, parsley, radishes, potatoes	beets, fennel, beans, peas, spinach, cucumber
carrot	onions, lettuce, beans, leeks, radishes, parsley, tomatoes, peas, chervil, garlic	beets, chard

Source: jardinactual.com/html/rinconverde/huerto/compatibilidad.htm (19-XI-2004)

The project of a garden

Shed
Here you can store garden tools, including the sprayer and, if there is enough room, the rototiller which—although it is not recommended because it pollutes the air—can help in large areas and assist people with physical difficulties. Also, you can make starter pots or store the recently purchased ones.

Pond

Here you can have a water source or a pond. It will be dedicated to clean carrots or to make strings of garlic.

Fruit trees and flowers

Here you could plant fruit trees, north of the rest of the garden if possible, to avoid casting shadows on other plants. You could also plant artichokes, beets, asparagus, culinary and aromatic plants, and flowering plants in order to attract insects. Roses are included, though you must be careful because they need sun and are very jealous of their private space. You could add blueberries, strawberries, and currants. If a cherry tree is planted it must be near the fountain or pond for irrigation. The garden will have good shade and splendid flowers in the spring.

Roots

In this area of the three-year rotation you will plant potatoes, carrots, parsnips, turnips, beets, and leeks.

Legumes

Here you can plant legumes for the three-year rotation: beans, peas, lima beans, and any other that makes a proper combination such as onions, garlic, lettuce, spinach, and radishes. On the edges you can plant chard, celery, and leeks. In the middle you can plant basil to ward off insects.

Cabbages

Here you can plant cabbages, cauliflower, broccoli, lettuce, and endive. You can plant tomatoes either here or in the legumes box.

Pumpkins

Here we can leave an area for plants that spread out, such as pumpkins, squash, cucumbers, or watermelons.

The garden, month by month

Below is a basic calendar, which applies to gardens in temperate regions (zones 7 and 8). Remember that growing seasons vary by climate, and you should refer to your seed packets for specifics.

In October

- If we have done well, the garden is still booming.
- You can still harvest beets, squash, cabbage, endive, spinach, lettuce, beets, and carrots.
- The time to let the garden rest is coming, although if the weather is good and the region is warm, we still encourage you to transplant onions, spring cabbage, endive, and strawberries, but it may be better to wait.
- Walnuts, hazelnuts, apples, and chestnuts are harvested.
- We add compost to soils that are becoming bare and begin to clean out the plants for winter.

In November

- Pull up annoying weeds, thoroughly stir the soil, add manure, and level the area you will use for sowing.
- Plant garlic, endives, spinach, lima beans, parsley, and radishes. If it is cold, use quick hoops (plastic tunnels).
- In a dry fall, water plants that are recently planted.
- You can already harvest onions, carrots, chicory, cabbage, and parsley. Regarding fruit crops, you can harvest quinces, pears, apples, oranges, and lemons.
- Apple and pear trees are pruned, fallen foliage is removed, soil is fertilized, and winter mineral oils are used.

In December

- It is probably the only month in which the everlasting chard is scarce, but if you have been prudent you will still have cabbage, endives, spinach, and carrots—not in cold weather though.
- In temperate zones we plant garlic, spinach, peas, and lima beans. We can also plant strawberries.
- Fertilize trees and start pruning.

In January

- Finish spreading the compost or manure and dig the ground deeply. If it is cold you should put mulch around the plants that are still green, like spinach.
- Harvest beets, broccoli, endive, spinach, escarole, cabbages, lettuce, and leeks.
- Sow in hotbeds: tomatoes, eggplant, and squash. If it is hot, plant peppers.
- Sow in single seedling pots: tomatoes, eggplant, endives, leeks, lettuce, celery, and early cabbage.
- Plant—outdoors—garlic, radishes, and carrots if the weather is warm.
- This is the ideal time to prune rose bushes and to plant pitted fruits. If you have vines you can dig them now.

In February

- Continue the work of the previous month if you have not finished all of it yet. The cold continues but in temperate zones you can transplant the seeds planted on hotbeds to starter pots or pots.
- Add green manure to the soil, weather permitting.
- We continue to harvest beets, cabbage, spinach, lettuce, endives, and turnips.
- You can also follow the same planting as in January but this time in a simple seedbed: chard, lettuce, endives, and leeks.
- Plant garlic, red beets, carrots, and radishes.

In March

- This is a month of climatic contrasts, so we have to be careful with the pots because frost could still occur. You must start preparing the soil in order to get going.
- Plant artichokes, cabbages, cauliflower, endives, peas, lima beans, leeks, lettuce, radishes, and carrots.
- Using covered seedbeds, sow eggplants, pumpkins, cucumbers, melons, and peppers.
- Using covered seedbeds, plant garlic, lima beans, spinach, potatoes, radishes, and carrots. If it is hot, also plant green beans.
- We start mulching with grass that has recently been cut.
- Plant mint and parsley. You can also plant rosemary from cuttings.
- You can transplant spring cauliflowers and leeks. Also, if it is hot or in coastal zones, you can plant tomatoes, zucchini, peppers, and eggplant, but use a lot of prudence.

In April

- This month you need to be really careful of late frosts, and the sowings you do will depend on location.
- The green manure will be ready for burial. We can sulfate with horsetail and sulfur to prevent pests.
- Continue the previous month's transplants, still keeping calm, because in inland areas the first days of the month it is still freezing.
- We enrich the compost and adjust the pH of the soil.
- Harvest artichokes, cabbages, spinach, chicory, lima beans, peas, lettuce, leeks, turnips, and carrots.

- Plant indoors: pumpkins, squash, melons, and cucumbers.
- In uncovered seedbeds, plant chard, celery, cabbages, and lettuce.
- Directly sow: squash, spinach, chicory, climbing beans, corn, turnips, potatoes, radishes, beets, and carrots.
- Transplant: onions, cabbages, lettuce, tomatoes (directly and protected), eggplant, squash, and peppers.

In May

- It is the best month. Vegetables and herbs grow joyously, so you will work to keep the garden clean in addition to a lot of harvesting and sowing that must be done.
- Harvest tender garlic, onions, celery, chard, broccoli, lettuce, turnips, leeks, small radishes, and carrots.
- In uncovered seedbeds, sow squash, cabbages, cauliflowers, melons, cucumbers, and leeks.
- Plant directly in the ground squash, pumpkins, onions, cabbages, melons, peppers, leeks, and tomatoes.
- If you have fruit trees, you may pick cherries and loquats.
- Insect prevention begins, such as against the fruit fly. It is time to prepare the traps.

In June

- The hot days start and we must be alert to watering. Tomatoes and squash require water but especially lettuces and endives that could potentially bolt.
- It is also the season of weeds, so you have to weed, especially if it has rained, and mulch generously to prevent them from growing.
- We continue harvesting chard, squash, celery, cauliflower, turnips, carrots, lettuce, and spinach. Add onions, strawberries, peas, tomatoes (in warm weather), potatoes, and beans.
- You can sow in uncovered seedbeds: fall and winter cabbages and cauliflower, endives, and lettuce.
- Plant beans, squash, short-cycle maize, beets, carrots, parsley, and radishes.
- Harvest all kinds of fruits. Plums begin.
- We bravely fight against the aphid.

In July

- It's too hot so you must water with drip irrigation or by furrows, but without wetting the plants. Mulch should cover everything. Select plants that will be used for seeds for the following year.

- Continue harvesting chard, celery, zucchini, cabbage, endives, spinach, lettuce, radishes, and beets. Add watercress, chickpeas, cucumbers, peppers, and eggplant. You can also add beans and tomatoes in cool climates.
- Directly plant beets, endives, spinach, and lettuce.
- Transplant celery, cabbage, and fall cauliflower.

In August

- It is really hot, the garden is at its peak, and it is the worst month to leave for vacation. You have to be there every day, because you have to pick and water daily. You will also need to give away or can the surplus—also a time-consuming task.
- Harvest basically everything except spring products such as artichokes, lima beans, peas, or spinach, although they endure cool climates.
- Directly plant chard, beets, endive, lettuce, and turnips.
- In seedbeds, prepare onions, lettuce, and cabbage.
- Transplant broccoli and fall cabbages.
- Continue to pick fruits: peaches, pears, plums, and the first grapes.

In September

- In some places, harvest will be diminished because sometimes August ends with rains and cool temperatures—though climate change has made some seasons longer.
- We continue harvesting, above all, tomatoes, cucumbers, eggplants, peppers, and beans (some of them already dry). However, spinach, cabbage, lettuce (already scarce when you crave it most), radishes, melons, watermelons, and carrots can also be harvested.
- Plant beets, celery (which is harvested almost all year round like chard), cabbage, spinach, endive, and lettuce.
- Transplant cabbage, onions, cauliflower, lettuce, endive, and leeks.
- It's the season for almonds. Table grapes are replaced with wine grapes. Persimmons ripen.

Harvesting
Vegetables

Vegetables: how to cultivate them, allies, and problems

A good garden requires time to reach its full potential. We will give you some ideas so you can enjoy waiting.

The moment of truth has come. The dream of every gardener is to supply him or herself with the basic, primal products while maintaining a rich and varied diet. You could say that every gardener is a gourmet and also an artist.

The first reason is that he or she must taste his or her own creations and judge for better or for worse—and he/she can always improve them. Do not just accept them as they are—the taste of onions or peppers not only depends on the type of seed and the fact that you fulfill the basic requirements of a good gardener. There are other factors such as type of soil, orientation, the shadow of a wall, an underground river, or even the love given to each plant.

Actually, we wanted to talk about the latter because a good gardener pampers his/her plants, puts all his/her heart into them, and is in some way linked to nature . . . and plants will thank him/her for this.

The good gardener ensures that the garden looks like a piece of art. Proportions are appropriate, the furrows are kept clean of weeds, the water falls and accumulates where it is supposed to do so, there are no harmful insects, the cat does not play in the bushes, and rabbits do not eat the sprouts because the gardener complied with his/her duties in a timely manner. There are no snails or slugs, or aphids, but ladybugs and birds. The soil is loose and its dark color stands out wherever it has not

been covered by dry leaves and herbs to prevent drying or weeds.

Leafy vegetables that we are going to eat—such as chard, spinach, or lettuce—do not have caterpillars. Not a single laboratory-produced chemical has been used.

If there is room, a good gardener has a few fruit trees; to eat an apple or a peach, all he/she needs to do is remove the dust by wiping it on her arm. Above all, a good gardener experiments, and since he/she is not stupid and wants to know what is the best way of doing things, he/she looks for and asks the older gardeners in the area. Yes, those who have spent many years doing the same as taught by their parents who in turn were taught by their grandparents. He/she learns from all of them and seeks ways to reproduce first, and to improve thereafter.

Do not be discouraged; a good garden needs time to reach full potential.

Leafy vegetables

Chard

Chard (*Beta vulgaris*) is a Mediterranean plant first described by Aristotle in the fourth century. It was a staple food for a long time due to its ability to grow anywhere and under all conditions. This is a biennial plant with a long cycle, very much like beets. The edible part is not the root but the leaves, which can reach large sizes.

Cultivation

Chard is a plant of temperate climates that freezes below 23°F (-5°C) and grows well between 43 and 86 °F (6 and 30°C). It does not need much light but does require enough moisture; this is noticeable in dry climates where it grows significantly in rainy seasons. It likes clay soil with a pH between 5.5 and 8. It tolerates salts pretty well, though not acids. It can be grown on ridges, leaving 16 or 20 inches (40 or 50 cm) between each plant. It can also be planted in pots, in an open and clean space. Place two or three seeds in each hole. Maturing period is 50 to 60 days. In warm weather they are planted throughout the year and in cold weather, from October to March; if done in seedbeds they are transplanted when they have 4 or 5 leaves in March-April. If sowing is done in pots, plastic sheeting can be used to cover the soil. Chard does not require an excessive fertilization, although in a manured soil it grows faster. Watering is recommended every 20 days at the most if it does not rain, but more abundant irrigation will also yield larger leaves. It blossoms the second year, and if allowed, its seeds are distributed so it easily grows in other parts of the garden.

Once flowered, you should pull it out and not plant it in the same place for two or three years. In the garden it goes well with low bush beans, carrots, and radishes.

Difficulties

Beware of slugs because chard's large leaves are usually very appealing to them. In this case they appear chewed on.

Aphids, cutworms, beet flies, and flea beetles can also attack. Excessive moisture can rot the leaves and cause other fungal diseases such as mildew, cyclospora, and beet mosaic. Lack of nutrients make the leaves look yellowish. Diseased leaves should be destroyed or burned. Leaves with gray spots should not be transplanted.

Usage

Biennial plant that blossoms every two years. Its leaves can be picked, depending on the weather, from three to six months of age. Chard is emollient, refreshing, digestive, diuretic, and nutritious. It is used against bladder inflammation, constipation, and hemorrhoids. In the kitchen it is used in salads, steamed or in the form of juice for intestinal diseases, and with lemon juice and olive oil to strengthen the stomach and stimulate the brain.

Varieties. Wild chard grows on the edge of fields and road. It is the tastiest, though it needs more cooking time. Moreover, there are many varieties: wide main rib, white or red, thin or narrow, dark or light green, curly or smooth . . .

Chard grows almost wild and reproduces well even in abandoned gardens.

TIP

In the garden, it goes well with celery, lettuce, and onions. Do not plant them with tomatoes.

Endive

Endives with Roquefort cheese

This is the most famous recipe.

● Wash the endives and place them in a dish, adding Roquefort sauce.

● For the sauce, simmer in a pot 3.5 oz (100 g) Roquefort cheese and 7 oz (200 g) of cream, and stir until thickened.

● Spread the sauce over the endives.

True **endive** (*Cichorium endive*) is the edible variety appropriate for the garden and is, in fact, a variety of chicory with a curly endive-like head and its inner leaves whitish.

Endive sold for consumption is grown using a technique called Witloof ("white sheet") so that its leaves do not receive light and acquire that commercial whitish tone you may be familiar with. The method for obtaining these Witloof endives is long and complicated for a family garden, as the ones intended for the store are the offspring of tender leaves that grow in the second year of its life cycle. The wild species has curled leaves and is very bitter to taste, but in the garden we find a substitute cultivating chicory or broadleaf endives. They are similar to lettuce,

Endive is also known as Belgian endive; this is not in vain, since Belgium and Luxembourg offer the greatest harvest around the world.

cold-resistant, and can be whitish if the leaves are tied together or put against each other, thus avoiding sunlight.

Properties

Endive–like chicory–is rich in fiber and regulates intestinal transit, cleaning bothersome substances from the digestive system. It protects the intestinal mucosa, prevents inflammation, fights gases and acidity, and last but not least, it basically has no calories, because its content is 94 percent water. It is also a diuretic and is used in weight loss recipes. Receiving no light, it lacks vitamin C, but it is antioxidant and anti-carcinogenic; meaning, in other words, it will extend your life.

Difficulties

Endive can be attacked by slugs and cutworms. Its common diseases are sclerotin and lettuce mildew.

TIP

Be careful when you eat endives to not leave them soaking in water because it accentuates the bitterness. Just pass them under cold water and drain before serving with a little oil or Roquefort sauce.

Curly Endive

Endive (*Cichorium endivia L.*) is a variety of endive, which in turn is a variety of chicory. It is believed to be native to India, but was already used in ancient Egypt and around the Mediterranean since time immemorial. Its leaves grow in a cluster without forming a floret. Inner leaves have a lighter color and are more attractive gastronomically because in addition to their curly shape—like the rest of the plant—they are slightly bitter and freshening. Curly endive is cleansing, laxative, refreshing, and contains vitamins A, B, C, and K. It also contains iron, magnesium, cobalt, manganese, and zinc.

Cultivation

Curly endive grows between 43 and 86°F (6 and 30°C) but can resist temperatures down to 21 °F (-6°C). It likes loamy, slightly acidic, rich in potassium, and well-watered soils with low humidity in the air. Heat causes it to bolt. Curly endive can be planted directly in the ground or in a seedbed at any time of the year. After a month it is transplanted to the ground. It is harvested after two or three months. It associates well with lettuce, carrots, beets, and cabbage.

Difficulties

Pests that usually attack curly endive are turnip moth, leafminers, whiteflies, Diptera larvae, caterpillars, aphids, leaf worm, thrips, snails, and slugs.

Lack of water will cause the tips of the leaves to seem burnt. Water them abundantly.

Bleaching the endive

Endive's green leaves are more bitter than the white leaves, which should not get any sunlight. In order to achieve this, **it is common to tie them with a rubber band or a cord so the inner leaves remain in the shade one week before harvesting.** It also helps when you grow them tightly close together, or when you cover them with planters fifteen days before picking. Some people do it with a black plastic tarp about ten days before harvest.

Varieties

There are two main types: Curly with very twisted and divided leaves, and escarole, with broad, wavy leaves and not so toothed. The latter are much more resistant to cold. The most popular varieties are: Agora, Brevo, Salonca, and Stratego, perhaps the best among the broad-leaved. Varieties for the curly ones are: Amel, Oxalie, Remix, and Tosca.

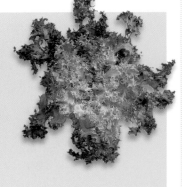

each other about 8″ apart. In rows around the garden they can be planted about 5 inches (12 cm) apart. The clove is buried about ¾ to 1⅕ inches deep (2 to 3 cm).

It can be planted in the Fall, between October and November, or even later, between December and January. In clay and wet soils it can be done between January and March. The tip is left upwards; be sure to choose the days of the waning moon, as in the case of other root crops.

Weeds should often be removed so the soil is clean. In general, it is not necessary to water them except when experiencing extreme dryness during head development period.

Harvest it eight months later if it has been planted in fall and four months if it has been done in spring, that is, between June and August in cold areas. Wait until the leaves are completely dry and the weather is dry to pick up the heads. If rain does not come its way for a while, you should leave those heads three or four days in the open, and then hang them on a string. They can also be harvested tender for tortillas before the bulb fattens. It gets along with strawberries, protecting them from diseases, and also with tomatoes, potatoes, lettuce, and beets. It does not like legumes.

Diseases

Excess moisture or fresh compost can cause fungal diseases. It can be affected by onion maggot, garlic and onion ringworm (*Lita allieta*), which bores the leaves and bulb, garlic weevil (*Brachycerus algirus*), which also pierces the bulb, moths that attack in June, and nematodes. Regarding diseases, it is sensitive to mildew, rust that yellows leaves, white rot, and botrytis.

There is no greater pleasure than putting garlic on a string after harvest.

A good **trick to have the best garlic crop** is to plant it three days after December's or January's full moon.

Putting on a string

To store garlic once dry and clean, tear off the outer leaves and with the inner ones make a braid in a chain and hang them on a dry place. This same technique is also common in the villages for onions and corn when they get dry.

Varieties

There is softneck and hardneck garlic. Hardneck varieties are known because they produce between 4 and 12 cloves, have a stalk with flowers, produce shoots, are difficult to put on a string because of the hardness of the stem, and rot quickly. Softneck or artichoke varieties do not produce shoots, have between 10 and 40 cloves forming layers, are easy to weave, and last for 6 to 8 months without getting spoiled once harvested. There is a variety called elephant (*Allium ampeloprasum*), related to celery, whose head can weigh up to 400 grams.

They take a while to grow, about six months, and are sown from the previous year's garlic cloves.

Celery

The origin of **celery** (*Apium graveolens*) is in the Mediterranean. It is an Umbelliferae that comes in two varieties: common celery (with edible leaves and stalks) and celeriac, or "turnip-rooted celery" (with an edible root). The first variety's leaves have a petiole (the plant part that connects the stem and leaves) of very thick, edible fleshy stalks. Celery requires deep, moist soil, which is neutral and rich in boron. If soil dries the plant becomes tough.

It has antirheumatic, carminative (intestinal gas releases), digestive, and diuretic properties. It is rich in vitamins A, B, and C, and has calcium, iron, magnesium, phosphorus, potassium, and sodium.

Cultivation

Celery's growing cycle is four months. Interestingly, this plant bolts when it's cold, so if the temperature drops in the summer it can be spoiled. It is sown in seedbed between July and August and transplanted between August and October, but can also be planted in a seedbed in November and transplant-ed in January and February. Soil temperature must not fall below 57°F (14°C). Transplantation is done two months later or when they are about 6 inches and have three or four true leaves, separating plants by about 1 foot. You should keep the ground free of weeds when celery is young because it grows very slowly and does not like competitors. You should water in abundance and with good water. It accepts sprinkler irrigation very well. You can earth up to whiten the leaves and they say that it is good to remove the soil around roots. It is harvested when it reaches the right size, in the morning or afternoon, not when it is hot. It is important to avoid the sun after cutting, to keep the leaves crunchy. It gets along with legumes, cabbage, cucumbers, tomatoes, lettuce, and radishes.

Problems

Carrot flies, whose larvae spoil the root. Celery flies, whose larvae attack the leaves. Aphids that bite the leaves. Nematodes that attack the root and prevent the plant from growing, such as cutworms that attack the root collar. Diseases that attack celery are mildew, blight, and septoria leaf blight—fungi that stain leaves.

Celery takes about three months to grow and is planted in the fall and winter because it has good resistance to frost.

A temperature drop or excess moisture or nitrates can hollow out the plant.

Black heart is formed by nutrient deficiency. If the plant lacks boron and magnesium, it will turn brown.

Strawberries

Wild strawberries and strawberries belong to the family Rosaceae, Fragaria variety. It is a herbaceous and perennial plant. The stem is formed by a short axis called a crown, in which leaves are inserted. Strawberries can sprout directly from the crown or from a leaf internode.

Generally, the ones that grow on the edge of the forest are called wild strawberries and the cultivated ones are strawberries, which are much bigger.

Strawberry is depurative, diuretic, laxative, and re-mineralizing. It has vitamins A, B, C, E, and K, calcium, bromine, iodine, iron, magnesium, potassium, etc. They are also often very digestive.

Cultivation

Strawberries prefer a mild climate. It grows wild in the mountains but crop varieties are more adapted to heat and constant moisture. It does not like drought and direct sunlight causes them to lose too much water so the leaves end up wilting.

If planting from seeds, you have to wait a year to have fruit. Typically planting is done from old bushes and there are two options. In the first one, the plant is pulled and its root divided, selecting the parts with new roots (the old parts are removed) and planted again. In the second option, stolons—those long twigs projecting strawberries and rooted elsewhere—are used. Once the root is grown, it is easy to pull them and take them elsewhere.

Once transplanted you have to water them often. If you live in a climate that frosts, dividing roots or transplanting stolons can be done to indoor pots after summer and transplanted back to the ground from April.

Strawberries like slightly acidic soil, and keeping them free of grass will give you some work. After four or five years you should pull all the strawberries and wait at least five years before planting again. Its root resists down to -4 degrees Fahrenheit but the leaves dry as frost begins. Strawberry gets along with garlic, legumes, spinach, and lettuce. It does not like cabbage.

Difficulties

Industrial crops are usually mulched with a black plastic. In the organic garden, chances are we have to pull weeds by hand. Strawberries form a roof of leaves that remains very damp so all kinds of animals grow under their shade. However, spider mites (which attack when there is drought), thrips, and aphids cause damage to the leaves. Attacks of snails and slugs are even worse, making ripe strawberries full of holes and unpalatable.

Excessive moisture can cause mildew or rot. Leaves turning yellow can also be a symptom of too much lime in the soil, which can be treated with pine humus.

Varieties

There are over a thousand varieties of strawberries.
The most widely grown variety in Spain is the Camarosa, designed at the University of California, which is sold in stores. For our garden, however, we have plenty of options, from creeping to climbing ones, and many different sizes.

Strawberries and snails

Snails are the greatest enemy that strawberry bushes may have. To prevent this, you will need to plant them on a straw or wood chips mulch. Snails will think twice before trying to eat strawberries, because they do not like the roughness and cutting edges of those chips at all. **For protection to be complete, we must ensure that the bushes are as clean as possible** and maintain moisture.

Melon

It is believed that the **melon** (*Cucumis melo*) originated in Africa, although it is likely that its varieties were improved in China and India. Later on, each country might have made their own selections, resulting in an amazing diversity that has been reduced to a few commercial varieties.

It is an annual plant, of the creeping or climbing type, that bears oval leaves with several lobes, toothed borders, and a hairy underside.

The first flowers to appear at the internodes are male and female, and hermaphrodite flowers will bud in the second or third generation of branches. The latter ones will lead to a varying shape and color fruit. Its rind may be smooth or ribbed. The seed appears in a gelatinous placenta located in a hole, in the center of the pulp.

Melon is a refreshing laxative, and diuretic fruit, rich in sugars, with vitamin A, B, C, and calcium, chromium, bromine, iron, phosphorus, as well as other minerals.

Cultivation

Melon is a plant of warm, dry climates typical to the Arab garden, scorched by the sun and properly watered. Hence, it is grown only in hot weather and Europe, except Spain, imports it from tropical countries. However, hybrid varieties grown withstand temperatures as low as 34°F. It grows in any soil, but better if it is well fertilized with well-rotted humus and after a deep dug soil.

In warm places, it grows all year, but in our latitudes it only does it in summer, so we will sow it directly between April and May and still cover the new seedling to avoid cold temperatures. The soil must be at least 61°F. Four or five seeds are placed in the hole and, once sprouted, one is allowed to grow.

If you are in a hurry, you can plant them in warm seedbeds in January or February and transplant them in May.

Some people have the habit, as they grow melons, of cutting the tips of the branches so that the nutrients are concentrated in the first fruits, since the last ones are smaller and only absorb energy from the plant. Watering must be abundant during the growth of melon, but you should avoid making the plant wet, and having puddles where the branches are supported. Especially, melons should be protected from contact with the ground with dry

In the kitchen, you can do wonders with melon, from smoothies to melon with ham or with clams, as well as soup, ice cream, and even melon stuffed with chicken.

straw or cardboard. They get along with corn, which in very sunny areas protects them from sunburn and does not reduce their nutrients. Otherwise, it gets along with other garden plants, except for the issue of the space, and it is better not to combine them with cucumbers or squash. Do not plant in the same place for three or four years.

Melons should be harvested at its peak ripeness in a garden, and the way to find out is the same you use when you buy them at the store. You must press the end and ensure that it is slightly soft and sinks a little, while the rest of the melon should be hard. Experience will soon teach you which ones are best.

Difficulties

Excessive moisture can cause mildew, cucurbit powdery mildew, fungi, gummy blight on the stem, and various viruses.

As for pests, although melon usually causes no problems, it has many enemies: spider mites, whiteflies, aphids, caterpillars, thrips, leaf miner, and nematodes. Sulfur should not be abused with melons because they do not like it too much. Other problems include: deformations in the fruit by poor pollination or lack of water; sunburn, which can cause white spots; cracked fruit, caused by lack of or excessive water; and brown spots on yellow melons caused by excessive moisture.

Honey Drew variety is a hybrid with a thick rind and long shelf life.

Plastic accelerator

Industrial crops use the black polyethylene to increase soil temperature and to prevent melons from touching the ground. **In order to accelerate production, little plastic tunnels are placed,** supported on archwires, to increase the temperature. A hive is also placed every half hectare so that bees pollinate the flowers.

Varieties

Melons can be divided by their shape or by their growing cycle; the best known are:

● **Yellow melons**, including the Canary and Golden, that have smooth skin, are more delicate, and have a three-month cycle.

● **The green melons**, involving three classes, the toad-skinned and **Rochet** (which are elongated, about 4 pounds, very sweet, and have a 100-day cycle) and the **Tendral**, which is thicker, with rough skin, low odor, native to Murcia, and with a four-months cycle.

● **The Cantaloupe melons**, that are round, small, yellow, sweet, and have a short three-month cycle.

● **The Galia melons**, which are very similar.

● **The Honey Drew**, which are yellow, with greenish flesh, and very sweet.

● There are shelf-stable varieties that only have an interest to market, designed in order to withstand long journeys.

Tomatoes

Sow tomatoes during the waxing quarter moon, and keep in mind that it gets along well with garlic, onions, carrots, leeks, parsley, and celery, and doesn't like potatoes, cucumbers, or kohlrabi.

In the photo to the right you have one of the numerous varieties of tomatoes, more than fifty, that there are in the world. Look for the one you like the best and plant them. To do so, ask veteran gardeners when their tomatoes are ripe and ask for a healthy one from which to get seeds.

The **tomato** (*Solanum lycopersicum*) is one of the most important crops in the world. It was first grown in the Americas, before the Spanish introduced it to Europe, and from there it spread around the world.

Properties

There are numerous varieties of tomatoes that adapt to the tastes and needs of each consumer or producer. There are large tomatoes to cut up for salads, medium ones for cooking or for making sauce, and small cherry ones to eat whole, which can be grown on a balcony or even on a windowsill.

In any case, the tomato has refreshing properties, it is a diuretic, it is calming and remineralizing, it is a great muscular tonic, and it purifies the liver. Eaten with the skin and the seeds, it is a laxative, and thanks to its lycopene content, it helps with rheumatism, stimulates the heart, and fights cancer. The tomato also has potassium (250 mg per 100 grams of tomato), copper, and vitamin C.

Soil and climate

The tomato grows in any type of soil, but it appreciates a well fertilized one with lots of humus. It tolerates salinity and the only thing that bothers it is puddling.

It is well known that when a wild animal eats a tomato, the seed perfectly withstands the trip through the digestive tract and can sprout from the excrement in any place, as long as it has enough moisture. It likes sun and hot temperatures, but it also grows in cool climates, as long as there is no frost. In very wet, cool climates, you can grow them in a greenhouse. Given that there are many varieties, there is not a single rule, but in general they need sun and heat to ripen. They don't like rainy summers, or excessive heat, above 105°F.

Fertilizer and watering

If you want to get a good crop, you should prepare the soil with a lot of compost or manure (6.5 pounds (3 kg) per square meter). It's best if legumes grew in that spot the year before. You should water abundantly, since the leaves fall off quickly if they lack water. It prefers regular watering, every two to three days, to heavy watering every seven or ten days. Water generously when the flowers appear, and then wait for ten days, earthing up the soil and weeding the rows. When it begins to produce fruit, resume regular watering, especially during harvest, since dry spells will stunt the growth of the fruit.

Sowing

Good gardeners select the best tomatoes each season for the following year. Select the thickest ones from the first crop. Let it ripen well and then open and extract the seeds, and dry them on a paper towel or newspaper.

Sowing can be done in hotbeds from February on, with a cover of glass if possible, which protects them from frost and retains heat from the sun.

On a well conditioned soil with humus, broadcast sow and cover with less than a centimeter of loose dirt. Water and thin when they have the first leaves, then strengthen the remaining plants. Some people sow in seedling trays, and others take advantage of a simple old container. When there is no longer danger of frost, transplant to the ridges, keeping the plants about 20 inches apart.

The hawthorn

The hawthorn is a good indicator that the frosts are over. When it flowers, you can transplant the tomatoes. Don't trust the almond trees, which can flower too soon.

A good stake or support is important when planting tomatoes, and in places where there is a risk of hail, some people cover them with a plastic netting. (See photo on page 187.)

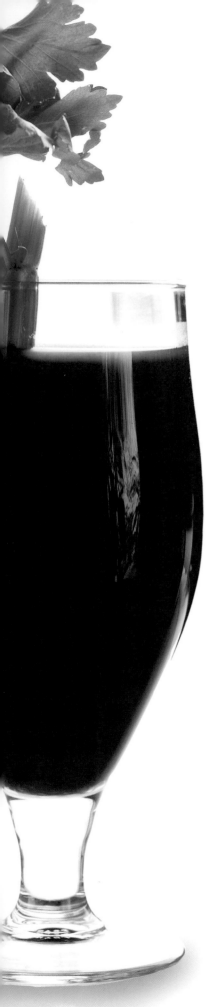

Growth

The tomato is one of the plants in the garden that needs the most care. You cannot leave it for more than a week in summer without suffering the consequences. In the first place, when it reaches a certain height, you will have to put in stakes to support the plant. The most common is to use three or four canes stuck in the dirt around the plant and tied together at the top to form a sort of teepee. Others prefer systems such as hazelnut branches, or even iron stakes, put in vertically with wires connecting the upper portion, like is done with fruit trees. There are also some who cover them with plastic to protect the tomatoes from hail. In order for the yield to be higher, it is good to remove the small secondary stems.

Pruning or Pollarding

During the growth, in the internodes of the stems, small sprouts appear, also called eyes, which should be removed about every ten days to thin the bush. If you don't do this, it will produce a jungle of leaves and smaller tomatoes. Pruning should be done from the top down. Some people only leave the main stem, but others leave various stems to obtain more tomatoes. Given that each master has his own notebook, you will have to trust experience, first that of the gardeners around you, and then your own.

Germination

The seeds of a tomato germinate in about six days, with a temperature of 75 degrees Fahrenheit, when planted in a seedbed with plastic or glass over to protect them.

Weeding, mulching, and defoliating

Unless you are making a Fukuoka-style garden, you should lightly dig the ground under the tomatoes to keep the soil loose and eliminate weeds. Mulching should be done when the plant is still small, laying a thin layer of peat or compost around to prevent the soil from drying too much. The tomato is like the palm tree—it wants to have its feet wet and its head dry and warm. In places where the sun is not strong, it is best to take some of the leaves of the plant, to prevent shadows, especially in fall, since the tomato continues producing fruits until the first frost, and from September on it is much harder to ripen.

The prince of tomatoes

In 1998, in the castle of Bourdaisiere, on the shores of the Loire, the **first Tomato Festival** was celebrated, sponsored by Prince **Louis Albert de Broglie**, a passionate gardener and horticulturist. He was also the creator of the brand **Le Prince Jardinier** of gardening tools and a defender of ecological gardening, which seeks to conserve the countless varieties of tomatoes that have been developed throughout European history. In the tasting in the castle, also sponsored by the **Tomato Conservatory**, more than four hundred varieties of tomatoes were displayed, with many recipes to bring out the flavor. Genetically modified, hybrid, or novelty varieties had no place in this festival.

Main varieties

● **Green tomato**: Contains consistent and fleshy pulp. It should be picked when it is just beginning to turn red, and is ideal for cutting up in salads or eating with oil.

● **Ripe tomato**: Smaller than the previous one, it is ideal for cooking, spreading on toast, or making gazpacho. It is an intense red color and very juicy.

● **Montserrat tomato**: It is aromatic and sweet, of a good size, not very productive but valued for its flavor. It is not very fleshy and has an irregular shape.

● **Vine tomato**: Similar to the ripe tomato, it is a little smaller and very round. You cut the whole little stem and can keep it for a few days.

● **Plum tomato**: It has the shape that its name indicates, is of medium size, and is very meaty. It is harvested when it is very ripe and ideal for canning.

● **Cherry tomato**: It is a very popular variety, genetically modified, of a size comparable to cherries, very aromatic, although sometimes very acidic. It is used in salads,

whole or sliced in half, and to decorate plates. A variety of this is the cherry vine tomato.

● **Raf tomato**: This is a variety of the Montserrat, but with more pulp.

There are more than a hundred varieties of accessible tomatoes; throughout the world there are more than ten thousand varieties, yet you only find two or three in the supermarket. The ones that you are going to plant, you should find them in a nearby place. Most of the time, a gardener friend will have a suitable variety near you. Don't disregard it, and don't hesitate to make your own seedlings.

Harvesting

Depending on the place and the plant, a tomato bush can produce many pounds of tomatoes. They are harvested two months after sowing, and until the cold prevents them from ripening or freezes them, although it depends on the climate and the variety. Some very early types stop producing quickly. The idea is to arrange to have tomatoes for the maximum amount of time by progressively planting from the last frost until May or June, and take care of the plants. Excessive defoliation reduces production.

As far as varieties, hanging tomatoes are good for winter.

Diseases

● **During transplantation**, the plants can be attacked by leaf worms, or cutworms, easy to discover because the plant dies. The best thing is to replace the plant, but first you have to find the worm and get rid of it. Cutworms are eliminated by burying slices of carrot and collecting them the next morning.

● **Powdery mildew** is a fungus that yellows the edges of the leaves, which die in the center. It is combated by clearing out weeds to prevent moisture and is killed with sulfur.

● **Gray rot,** or botrytis, produces lesions on the tomatoes and they end up rotting. It is detected by the white mycelium. It is combated by cleaning the soil and stem, so that it is well ventilated, but it is difficult to get rid of.

● **Excess moisture gives rise to mildew,** a fungus that causes irregular, greasy-looking stains on the leaves, which necrotize little by little. The same thing happens on the stem and the tops of the fruits, with brown spots that end up rotting. You must get rid of the sick parts, not wet the plant, and apply Bordeaux mix when the plant is young, or sulfur. If the weather is wet, it is best to do this before the disease appears.

● **White rot** is a fungus that appears on the stem or leaves, detected by its abundant mycelium. It is fought with cleaning and sulfur, like botrytis.

● **Other fungi that attack the tomato** are Alternaria, *fusarium, verticillium*, and root fungi, which mainly affect the seedlings before transplanting. In all cases, avoid excess moisture and weeds at the base of the plants, since that's where the enemy hides.

● **Bacterial diseases are chancre**, black stain, or scabies, and soft rots; in the first case, the lower leaves wilt, in the following, black spots appear, and in the last one, a watery and bad smelling rot. In all cases, it is combated by using healthy seedlings, not injuring the stem of the adult plant (easy to do when tying or pruning), avoiding excess moisture, eliminating sick plants or fruits, and treating the plants with copper.

• **The viruses** can be of various classes, from the tomato-spotted leaf virus, the mosaic virus, the potato virus, the yellow leaf curl, or the tomato bushy stunt virus. In the first and last cases, the plant does not grow, in the case of the mosaic, potato virus, and bushy stunt, yellow stains appear on the leaves, and in the case of the leaf curl, the leaves are smaller. They are combated by eliminating affected plants, removing weeds, and using resistant varieties, something that you will only discover through experience.

More common problems

• **Rotting at the base of the fruit** is very common, especially from September onward. It can happen due to lack of water, excess of salt, lack of calcium, or unexpectedly cold nights.

• **Splits** are deep cracks that appear on the surface of the tomato from the stem. It is caused by irregular watering, poor fertilization, and sudden cold spells.

• **Sunburn**, can make whitish splotches appear on the fruits and cause them to rot quickly.

• **Lack of nitrogen** produces weak, yellowed leaves.

How to remedy the loss of copper in tomato plants

During the period of growth, tomato plants require supplemental copper. Commercial products can be a great help. However, **you can use a very simple and economical home remedy.**

• **Take a rigid copper wire for electrical conduction,** cut it into 16-inch (40 cm) pieces, and remove the protective plastic coating.

• **Once clean,** stick them in the ground about 8 inches (20 cm) from the tomato plant. Each plant needs four pieces.

• **With the same pieces of copper,** you can also make rings to place around the bush. You must place them on carefully, without damaging the stem, and separated by about 4 inches (10 cm).

Lycopene

The color of the tomatoes indicates that it possesses one of the most interesting pigments that exist in foods, lycopene, the carotenoid that gives them their characteristic red color. **Ten or more weekly servings of foods rich in lycopene**—watermelon, tomato sauce, red grapes, red grapefruit—**contributes to reducing the risk of certain types of cancer, especially prostate, pancreatic, lung, and colon cancer**. It has also been shown to improve the immune system, like the rest of the foods that contain carotenes, such as carrots. Curiously, **blood plasma absorbs lycopene better when it comes from products made at high temperatures** than it does from fresh tomatoes. Tomato sauce is one of the best sources of lycopene, especially when consumed with a little olive oil.

• **Lack of magnesium** causes yellowed leaves with brown spots that you must spray with magnesium sulphate.

• **Lack of phosphorous** makes the flowers dry out.

• **Lack of potassium** makes the leaves curl at the edges, not grow, and yellow.

• **Lack of manganese** makes the leaves whitish along the veins.

• **Lack of copper** can be compensated for by placing pieces of copper near the trunk of the tomato to reinforce its growth.

In all cases, you must fertilize the plant well and water it judiciously, or the harvest will be at risk.

Ripe tomatoes keep better if you keep them upside down, and apart.

Flower crops

Artichokes

The **artichoke** (*Cynara scolymus*) is a perennial plant that can grow up to five feet and sprouts each year after winter. A derivative of cardoon, it originates in North Africa, and the species were selected locally. With cardoon, you harvest the leaves, whose meaty ribs are edible. The artichoke develops a rosette of narrower leaves and the edible part is the flower, covered in membranous, overlapping scales (bracts), meaty at the base, which is what you eat.

The first producer in the world is Italy, followed by Spain. Artichokes possess anti-anemic properties, stimulate hunger, favor the evacuation of bile, are purifying, stimulating, contain vitamins A, B, an C, and have phos-

phorous, magnesium, and calcium.

Cultivation

The artichoke is a winter crop that grows well between 45 and 85°F (7 and 30°C).

The cold induces flowering, but when the fruit is not formed, frost is not good for it. It likes deep, well fertilized soils, slightly alkaline. It tolerates salinity. It does not like a humid climate, but likes moist soil. Like cardoon, it does very well with drip irrigation. If not, use irrigation by furrows.

It can be planted from seeds, although the wait until harvest will be about eight months to a year, or through shoots or cuttings, which shortens the process to four or five months. The shoots, also called suckers or runners, are picked in February or March; cut leaves and roots and plant them in greenhouses until they take root and then return them to the garden. Cuttings are taken from the mother plant in summer, and planted directly, preferably in a waxing quarter moon. The plants produce artichokes for two years, and after that they are small and not very meaty. It's best to replace half the bushes each year, to have artichokes that are in their first and second years.

The harvest begins in October, and if the weather is good, it can last until May of the following year. The cone of meaty bracts is the flower that is collect-

ed before it ripens, keeping in mind that the first few picked will be bigger than the later ones. Lack of water will make them open and dry out too early. They should be cut 3 or 4 inches (8 or 10 cm) below the flower, in a way so that the stem remains a little below the lateral flowers. It associates well with lettuce, cabbage, onions, and legumes, but it prefers to be alone due to its size.

Difficulties

It is less tolerant than cardoon, and if left alone will produce small, hard artichokes. If it is watered too much or has too much nitrate, it is attacked by army worms, which attack the stem, leaf miners, and many types of aphids, some hidden in the folds of the main nerve. It is also victim to snails, artichoke moths, and various beetles. Heat and humidity provoke the attack of mildew and so-called artichoke grease, which causes stains in the bracts.

The main producer of the artichoke in the United States is California, where, since 1949, they celebrate the Artichoke Festival, where Marilyn Monroe was the first Artichoke Queen.

weather, leave them out for a few hours in the fresh air, covering the piles with burlap so the sun does not hit them. Then store them in a dry place, in the shade and in an area as cool as possible, as long as it is not less than 40°F.

After planting potatoes in an area, it is best to wait three or four years before repeating. They associate well with cabbages, spinach, and beets, and they don't like tomatoes.

Difficulties

The main problem is the potato beetle, a round yellow or reddish beetle with black stripes, introduced from the United States. It lays orange eggs on the undersides of leaves, and between the larvae and caterpillars, they finish off the aboveground part of the plant. This diminishes production, but not quality.

The most ecological way to fight them is by hand, pulling off the worms and squashing the eggs, even if you have to do it daily.

There is a very effective and simple way to get rid of potato beetles: plant chamomile between the rows. You will see how it scares off worms.

The cut worm attacks from below, making holes in the tubers. There is also the cabbage moth, various aphids, nematodes, fleas and flea beetles, and potato moths, which attack the piles after they are har-

From the roots of the **Jerusalem Artichoke** we obtain a high-quality alcohol.

Jerusalem Artichoke

Helianthus tuberosus, also known as sunroot or earth apple, is a perennial plant, whose underground roots grow tubers that are eaten cooked. They have a flavor similar to artichokes and tend to ferment, producing gas in the intestine (which is why it is sometimes also called the fart potato), but it is considered an aphrodisiac, and a diuretic, and a substitute for potatoes for diabetics. It reproduces from the tubers underground, and can be left year after year and it will grow again in spring. It is undemanding, and grows well with clover. It is also used to fatten livestock, with the stems and leaves making good forage, and fermented alcohol from the stems is very high quality.

vested. In wet seasons, you may also encounter mildew, some viruses, and fungi such as early blight, which is an alternaria. To avoid these kinds of problems, water with a purine of nettles. In industrial farming, they cover the soil with plastic to prevent weeds; you will have to prevent weeds by weeding and using a light mulch of straw or dry grass clippings.

Any of these afflictions is worsened by excessive moisture, but you also have to be careful of the sun, since if it

touches the tubers, they will turn green and be ruined.

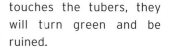
Potatoes grow wild in the high Andean plateaus and are fundamental to the survival of the population in some regions.

The potato on the balcony

You are dealing with a plant that occupies very little space to the sides, but that can grow very deep under the soil, which is what they prefer, and produces an enormous number of potatoes (unlike the sweet potato, which does not produce more than four per plant). It is not unusual for a plant to produce twenty or thirty potatoes. So, if you construct a box about 20 inches high, you can plant as many potatoes as will fit across its width. To get an idea of the size, take a look at the ideal system of permaculture, which consists of stacking two to four tires and filling them with well-fertilized earth. The tires help retain moisture. **In any case, you can obtain quite a few pounds of potatoes with a good tub in the corner of your balcony.**

Legumes

Peas

Originating in the Far East, perhaps Persia or India, and as ancient as lentils—since they were already known in prehistory—peas (*Pisum sativum*) were brought to Europe by the people who lived in the Iranian plateaus. In Rome, they were fed to horses. In the 15th century in Europe, they were eaten dried and cooked with bacon, and they were not eaten green until the 17th century, first in Holland, then France, and then Italy. In central Europe, it's common to eat them when very tender.

The main producer worldwide is India, with

ately, as often is or should be done in industrial agriculture.

They are very rich in sugar and carbohydrates, easier to digest than other legumes, and very nutritious. They are often accompanied by other foods, although they are also very good by themselves.

Harvesting is done when the pod is formed, before it begins to dry. Pull the pods off once they have grown fat, and then open them with a fingernail and extract the peas. Once dry, peas are very good for making compost, and there are even varieties for animal feed. After a couple of

Peas and fava beans are the only legumes that can be eaten raw when picked fresh and tender from the bush.

about four million tons, followed by China, the United States, and France. The pea is a climbing legume, with tendrils to support it up to six feet high. In the crux of the leaves appear one or two flowers, which produce the pods of about 2 to 4 inches (5 to 10 cm), with up to a dozen round seeds. These seeds are very sweet when freshly picked, although in about 20 minutes the sugars transform into starch and it is not as satisfying to eat them raw. You can also freeze them immedi-

Varieties

Peas can be divided according **to shape or color of the seed, the size of the plant, or the use of the product**— this last one is of most interest to us, since there are those for conserving and freezing, for direct consumption, and for consuming the pod before the seeds fully develop.

years, you can plant them in the same spot again. Except for garlic and onions, they get along with all the other plants in the garden.

Cultivation

The pea is a warm-climate crop, which grows between 42 and 95°F, withstands mild frosts, and prefers to be between 60 and 68°F. They like well fertilized clay soil with a pH between 6 and 6.5. Given that it is a spring plant, it probably does not need to be watered.

In mild climates, it can be sown in fall and harvested in early spring, although the most common is to plant them at the end of winter and harvest them in late spring.

They are planted directly in the ground, about 2-2.5 inches (4 to 5 cm) deep, or on top of the soil and covered with wood chips to protect them from frost and keep them moist, in rows about 12 to 20 inches (30 to 50 cm) apart, depending on the variety. When they sprout and are about 4 inches (10 cm) tall, weed thoroughly if you have not mulched. Since it is a very tender plant and

Lentils

The lentil (*Lens esculenta*) originated in Southeast Asia or Mesopotamia, and from there spread through Europe. It is mentioned in the Iliad, and seems to have saved Europe from famines during the Middle Ages. **Today, its main producers are Turkey and India.**

It is a free-standing plant, with a maximum height of about 20 inches (50 cm). The leaves are made up of 15 leaflets around a rachis. **The small flowers are found in a floral peduncle, which produces a diamond-shaped fruit with two lentils inside.**

Among the varieties, notable ones are the Armuña, pardina, verdina, and the biggest, the Laird lentil.

They are rich in protein and iron, and in mild climates they are grown in winter, since they are a cool-weather plant, but they do not like extreme cold or heat. **The lentil is generally an industrial crop, which is not worth the effort in a garden, but you can still do it: plant in October in rows about 12 inches (30 cm) apart, leaving an inch or two (3 to 5 cm) between the seeds.** It is a dry crop, so you don't need to water it. It should be harvested in June or July. In the fields, they used to do this with a scythe when the plant was yellow, and then they threshed them and cleaned them. You can do it by hand, but in a small garden, you will hardly get a plateful. They can be attacked by aphids and weevils, and if it is wet, also by some fungi.

very attractive to birds, until they are about 8 inches (20 cm) tall you should protect them with a netting or some other system designed to keep hungry critters away. Otherwise, you will have to get up very early to chase them away. In climbing varieties, you should put in stakes or supports so that the tendrils grab on, whether they are canes, sticks, or iron.

Difficulties

In addition to birds, snails and slugs like the tender leaves of the sprouts. Once they have grown, they can be attacked by aphids, beetles, thrips, and pea moths or their larvae (*Laspeyresia nigricana*), a moth that lays eggs on the leaves and whose caterpillars go into the pods, then the peas, and eat them from the inside.

Fava beans

Fava beans can be picked while tender, before the seed has fully developed, if you want to eat the shells, or when the bean is still green in the pod.

The **fava bean** (*Vicia Faba L.*) is a plant that originated in the Near East, but spread rapidly through the Mediterranean region. The Romans selected the species of large, flattened beans that are recognized today.

This is a leguminous plant whose fruit is a legume (in the form of a pod) that can be up to 14 inches (35 cm) long. You can eat the pod and the bean together, when the legume is tender, or just the bean, when it is ripe.

The fava bean is rich in phosphorous.

The main producer of fava beans is Algeria (125,000 tons), followed by China, Cyprus, Morocco, and Spain.

Cultivation

The fava bean is not very demanding, although it prefers mild, coastal climates. It does not sprout above 68°F and does not ripen at more than 86°F. It likes clay or siliceous soils, and if they are limestone, it must be rich in humus and well drained. Its ideal pH is between 7.3 and 8.2.

For planting, the soil should be deeply dug. The seeds are buried every 10 to 12 inches (25 to 30 cm) in ridges or rows about 20 to 24 inches (50 to 60 cm) apart. They sprout after 8–12 days and are harvested in three months. They can be planted from September to November for early varieties, and in spring in cold climates. It is good to fertilize with manure. The roots of the fava bean have a symbiotic bacteria, *Rhizobium leguminosarum*, which fixes nitrogen in the soil and benefits other crops.

Difficulties

It is often attacked by a parasitic plant called bean broomrape (*Orobanche crenata*), which is combated by crop rotation, eliminating affected plants, or pulling them out by hand.

The most common pest is the black bean aphid, which causes the leaves

Chromotropic trap

This is a yellow **sheet that you hang from a nearby tree or pole, which is impregnated with a pheromone substance** and an adhesive substance. You can also try fly traps made from a plastic bottle cut in half, with the top part inserted into the bottom part. By planting nasturtium, you will keep out ants, which carry aphids.

Varieties

● **Aquadulce or Sevillana**, an early variety with large pods that take 6 to 7 months to ripen, although you can pick them earlier to eat.

● **Granadina**, is the most tolerant of cold.

● **Mahon blanca or morada** is sensitive to cold, but resistant to drought; it produces narrow pods.

● **Muchamiel** is called the "forty-something", since it can be eaten forty days after sowing.

to curl and produces a honeydew that favors the presence of fungi. It is fought by keeping the soil clear of weeds, with yellow chromatic traps, or by taking them out by hand.

The sitona (*Sitona lineatus*) is a beetle that chews on the leaves in its adult stage, and attacks the nodules of Rhizobium as larvae. The pea thrip (*Kakptrips robustus*) gives the leaves a silvery appearance.

The diseases of the fava bean are mildew, rust, and botrytis (reddish brown tips or spots), always in the case of excessive moisture.

fruit trees

A brief introduction
to fruit trees

At a country house, any corner is good for a fruit tree: at the edges of the garden, along paths, in little-used corners, along an irrigation channel, by a pond . . .

The cherry tree by the acequia

Fruit trees are an accessory to the garden that you will really appreciate at harvest time. I will never forget the first garden I knew in my childhood. A huge cherry tree shaded the reservoir that the gardener used to irrigate. With great skill, he watered beans, tomatoes, peppers, and eggplants by conducting the water through furrows, in those summers that expired on the 15th of September, when climatic changes brought on the long autumn and made spring a treacherous friend.

A shadow in the garden

Most gardeners don't like the shade of the trees, or their roots. There are trees that are not permitted near a garden: poplars and shaking poplars have very shallow and extensive root systems that impede the growth of plants; pines acidify the soil around them and their shade is perennial. There are trees that get along well with uncultivated corners: the cherry, a walnut beside the fountain, a fig tree against the wall, a pear tree over the garden bench, with the bundle of canes you will use for the beans and tomatoes leaning against it.

To reinforce the immune system of fruit trees, you can add minerals to the base of the trunk.

In small gardens, it's not unusual to see delicate peach trees and wizened olives accompanying the work of the gardener, as well as vines, among which you can plant melons or squash. Beans grow well at the feet of olive trees, and even gain protection from intense frosts. Under peach trees, you can plant early lettuce or peas, and even garlic and strawberries grow well under the trees, but the rest of the crops prefer to be far away, in a corner where their sunlight is uninterrupted.

The climate

In countries like El Salvador or Guatemala, which are in the tropics and have mountains that produce every climate, the list of fruit trees grows considerably. For example, at sea level, you can plant avocados, custard apples, myrtle, coconut, guava, plums, lemons, cashews, mangoes, macadamias, papayas, pineapples, tamarinds, and sapotas, all trees that are impossible to grow in a temperate-Mediterranean climate, for example. Even oranges need to be grown higher than 300 meters, and as you go up you will find loquats, mandarins, mameys, plums, cherries, figs, blackberries, and peaches. In any case, the climate is a determining factor for fruit trees. The Chinese that introduced the lychee to the Mexican state of Sinaloa knew this well, since this state has a climate similar to the southeast of China, from where the plant originates.

Keep in mind that there are species that need the winter cold to bear fruit, that is, a certain number of hours at below 45°F (7°C) for the tree to grow fruit, depending not just on the species but the variety. In general terms, almonds, hazelnuts, peaches, quince, Japanese plums, figs, and grapes need less than 100 hours; apples and pears need more than 200, although they do best with more than 600 hours; a minimum of 300 for the apricot tree; 400 for the walnut; 500 for the cherry; and 800 for the European plum. Except for the almond, the apricot, the quince, and the fig, most trees do better with at least 1,000 hours of winter cold below 45°F (7°C) during the three winter months. Therefore, this kind of tree is found inland, with oranges and lemons on the coast, as they don't need any cold (although they tolerate near-freezing temperatures and grow well in tropical regions).

Conditions for growing

Fruit trees are permanent plants, although some last more than others, from the ten years of a peach tree to the hundred years of a walnut. You have to keep this in mind when choosing the placement. Also keep in mind that the soil must be deep, with more than a meter of soil before reaching the bedrock. The fig tree likes to be beside walls or fences, which retain moisture longer. The majority of species need good drainage. In sandy soils you will have to water much more frequently than in clay soils with a lot of organic material. To make sure the yield is sufficient, the trees need enough water. You also have to keep in mind the risk of diseases. There are species that are more sensitive than others, like peaches, which get sick easily and require more care.

The wind

Fruit trees don't like too much air, and so they grow best when protected by a wall or in an inner patio, or behind the house, sheltered from wind. Some people plant big trees to protect them, although the most common in this area is not barriers of fir trees but rather cypresses; you can plant many flowers at the base of them.

Trees and the climate

The mango is a type of fruit that is reproduced through grafting, since planting the fruit does not produce enough quality.

In cold northern countries, they can only enjoy a few species of trees that produce nuts: walnuts, chestnuts, hazelnuts, and beechnuts. In the Mediterranean and other subtropical regions, there are countless species and varieties you can grow.

Fruits of very temperate climates

These trees are not very tolerant of frost and especially not in the spring, once they have flowered. The temperature should not go below 28°F (-3°C). When they are grown inland, you will need to protect them from late cold snaps, using smoke to produce artificial fog:

Lemon, mandarin, orange, grapefruit, prickly pear, palm, and banana trees.

Fruits of somewhat temperate climates

These species tolerate frost well, not so much in late spring, but they need a lot of sun and not a lot of fog. The temperature can go below 23°F (-5°C) on occasion, but persistent or colder spells will freeze the trees:

Apricot, mesquite, almond, persimmon, pomegranate, fig, jujube, kiwi, loquat, olive, and stone pine trees.

Fruits of cold climates

Fruit trees specific to climates with freezes in winter, spring, and fall, which need cold and tolerate late frosts to a certain point. It is not unusual for the temperatures to go below 15°F (-10°C):

Blueberry, hazelnut, chestnut, cherry, raspberry, gooseberry, plum, apple, quince, peach, nectarine, walnut, pear, and grape vines.

Fruits from hot climates

List of the most common species that grow in the tropics. They do not tolerate frost at all.

● **Jackfruit**	*Artocarpus integriflora*
● **Avocado**	*Persea americana*
● **Cacao**	*Theobroma cacao*
● **Coffee**	*Coffea arabica*
● **Coconut**	*Cocoa nucifera*
● **Cherimoya**	*Annona cherimolia*
● **Guava**	*Psidium guajaba*
● **Lychee**	*Litchi chinensis*
● **Mango**	*Mangifera indica*
● **Papaya**	*Carica papaya*
● **Pineapple**	*Ananas cosmosus*
● **Rose apple**	*Eugenia jambos*
● **Tamarind**	*Tamarindus indica*

Citruses   Orange

Oranges, mandarins, lemons, and grapefruits originated in Asia. With the conquest of Alexander the Great, the first specimens of lemon trees came to Europe (*citrus* comes from the Latin for lemon), and with time, oranges appear with all their variations, until the 19th century, when the delicious mandarins arrived.

Citruses originated in the subtropical and tropical regions of Asia, from which they have spread all over the world. Of all the varieties, the orange is the most common, and of all the types, the Valencia orange is the most sold, followed by the Navel. The orange tree is a perennial tree with simple, coriaceous leaves, and white, aromatic flowers, called azahar, which give off an unmistakable aroma in the spring. It is so fragrant that it is worth including one in your garden just for that reason, as long as you live in an area that does not get too many frosts, and that does not go below 25°F (-3°C) after January, when they flower.

Others

● **Mandarins, grapefruit, and lemons** follow the same guidelines, although lemons tolerate more heat and mandarins tolerate more cold.

● **The mandarin** has been generally displaced by the clementine, which is easier to grow commercially.

● **The lemon** is reproduced through grafting onto the trunks of bitter oranges, and like orange trees, you can always graft new varieties when they are adults.

Cultivation

The orange tree likes deep, clay soils that are well-drained, without too much calcium or sodium, and it needs abundant watering to be sweet. Normally, you buy a young plant and plant it in the garden. After that, you can graft to improve it. If you want to grow one from a seed, the process is complicated. Plant the seed in a seedling pot, and when it is about 8 inches (20 cm) tall, move it to a protected covering on the ground, keeping the plants a meter apart, where they will remain for at least a year. After that, transplant them to the garden, and it will take 6 to 8 years for them to produce fruit.

They require quite a bit of fertilizer and it is best to use drip irrigation to save water, although many gardeners use flood irrigation every ten to fifteen days.

Pests include ants, aphids, and mealybugs, and

Loquat

The loquat originates in Southeast Asia and entered Europe as an ornamental tree. Tall, it can reach up to 35 feet (10 m) in the best of cases. It is distinguished by its large,

Underground pruning

If the fruit trees grow and produce too much wood—that is, grow too many branches—you can **cut one or two thick roots near the trunk.** This way, the tree will be weakened and can be controlled, and floral **buds will sprout from the wood buds.**

perennial leaves—coriaceous, spear-shaped, and hairy. The flowers are white and fragrant, and flower from the previous year's branches. They flower at the end of fall or winter, and the fruit ripens in April to June. The fruit is small, about 2 inches (5 cm) in diameter, and has various large seeds that are very flavorful.

It is a tree of temperate climates, that does not need cold—the frost harms the fruit. The main producer is Japan, followed by Brazil, **Algeria**, and India.

It is reproduced by grafts on hybrids and quince trees.

Pruning is best done in a pyramid shape, and you should thin the fruit when they are a little bigger than a hazelnut.

Flowering branches

In maintenance pruning with stone fruit trees, certain terms come up a lot: for example, flowering branches are those on which the flowers appear. **They are new branches, between 6 and 12 inches (15 and 30 cm), which have the flower buds. They are so delicate, that in peach, nectarine, and some apricot and plum trees, if you let it, the weight of the fruit will break them, and so it's best to prune them.** Chifonas are even smaller branches, long and weak, which must be pruned from the base, but in cherries and almonds, leave the strongest ones and cut the rest off, because the fruit does not weigh as much.

Mixed branches are about 12 inches to 36 inches (30 cm to 1 m), and have flower and wood buds (from which new leaves will sprout). **These are pruned two different ways: French style**, leaving some mixed branches and cutting others off at the second bud—the next year eliminate the mixed branches and leave the ones that were pruned; and **American style**, leaving very long branches so that they bow with the weight of the fruit and produce new branches near the base, which will be the ones you leave for the following year.

Wood branches and water shoots, which don't produce flowers, should be eliminated, unless you need to fortify the tree by lopping off the woody branches.

degrees Celsius) and a deep, clay soil with sufficient moisture.

They reproduce through seeds and grafts onto hybrids or quince. The most

Pear trees are grown on rootstock of quince, since this makes the trees smaller and more accessible.

which, like the others, produces fruit in October. Pruning should be limited to thinning the branches, since it is a slow-growing plant that does not have

Seeded fruits

Apple, quince, and pears have an endocarp that

Apple trees

Golden Delicious, whose fruit is large and golden yellow, and harvested in early fall; **Red Delicious**, whose

Other trees

Here we will briefly review some of the varieties not included in the previous three categories, but that are common in gardens.

Plastering the trees

Often trees have wounds to the trunk that can get infected or attract parasites. **To prevent any cuts or scratches from harming the tree, you can prepare a putty of polymer clay, manure, and fine sand, mixed in equal parts, with which you will cover the trunk, branches, and sprouts.** In the case that you have many trees, you can use 80 percent clay and 20 percent manure. It is best to apply this mixture in fall, after all the leaves have fallen, or at the end of winter or early spring.

Almond tree

It is originally from Central Asia, from which it reached Persia and Mesopotamia and Spain two thousand years ago. It has a smooth trunk that grows rough over the years, with greenish bark when young that turns brown to gray as it ages. The flowers are formed on flowering branches mostly and appear when the cold sets in. The fruit is a long-lasting drupe, and is one of the most valued nuts. It requires cross-pollination to bear fruit, done by bees, like in cherries. A single tree will not bear fruit. It does not like late frosts, and blooms too early, so that sometimes the crop is lost. They reproduce by grafting on host stock of almond, peach, or plum (the latter in wet climates). Among the many varieties, some notable ones are: the Marcona, with a rounded shell, Desmayo Largueta, with elongated fruit, the Desmayo Rojo, with thick fruit, Guara, Cristo Morto, Garrigues, Moncayo, etcetera. Almond trees are grown in dry areas, so you don't need to water, but if done, it increases production. Pruning is done in the vase shape, but can also be done on a trellis against a wall.

Hazelnut

Originally from Asia Minor, it was introduced to Europe by the Greeks. It is believed that the name comes from the city of Avella, Italy. It is a tree of no more than 15 feet high, quite irregular in shape, with many branches coming from the trunk. When young, the branches are quite straight, as anyone familiar with the practice of detecting water with a hazel wand knows well, and when they are old they become twisted. The leaves are large and round and the result is a cup-shaped achene.

It grows in temperate climates. It needs at least 700 hours below 45 degrees Fahrenheit (7 degrees Celsius), but can be found anywhere from near the coast to 1,500 meters above sea level in the Pyrenees mountains, where it bears excellent fruit. It likes moisture and rich, deep soils, and if it lacks water, it will drop the fruit. The main producer is Turkey, followed by Italy, the US, Spain, Azerbaijan, China, and Iran. It breeds in many ways: by seed, cutting, layering, stake, and graft (bud or approximation). The varieties are numerous, and it is best to find one adapted to the place where you want to plant. Pruning is done to favor new growth, in which the fruit appears in the following year.

Chestnut

Like the walnut tree, you can cultivate this tree for shade or fruit. Its origin is in Eastern Europe. It is a large tree, with spear-shaped leaves, an upright trunk, and a leafy canopy, which blooms from May to June. It is happiest in the mountains, between 500 and 1,200 meters of altitude, especially in wet places sheltered from excessive sun. If you want to have it as a fruit tree, you must pollard it to about 6 feet tall when the trunk is about 3 in (7 cm) in diameter, so it will grow side branches.

Walnut

Olive

Grapevine

Originally from Persia, it is even bigger than the chestnut tree and is sensitive to late frosts, which can easily kill the new buds and leave the tree in a very sorry state. It is propagated by grafting, and grows well along rivers, where it has plenty of water, since like the chestnut, it needs more than 260 gallons (1,000 liters) of rain per year.

It is believed that the olive comes from the eastern coast of the Mediterranean and that the Phoenicians were those charged with taking it to Greece and Italy, where it spread across the world, introduced by the Spanish to Peru, Mexico, and California. Many gardeners have received land that was an olive grove before and still have been able to plant garlic, beans, peppers, and tomatoes at the base of the trees, since the old olive tree is deeply rooted and earth can be worked and composted around the tree, pruning well to not block the sun. The oil is the juice from the fruit, but to be profitable, you must have an olive grove. However, with one or two trees, you can have olives for quite some time. If left to grow freely, *Olea europaea* can reach a significant size, as occurs in gardens where the gardener waters a lot but is not skilled. The tree has a smooth and crooked trunk, and over the years acquires fantastic shapes that make it very attractive. It is also attractive because of its small, pointed leaves, gray-green in color and very dense. The fruit is a dark drupe when ripe and green when unripe. It does well in limestone soils, and likes the light. It does not need watering and tolerates cold as low as 15 degrees Fahrenheit (-10 degrees Celsius). If it freezes, suckers sprout, and when it needs water, it may lose fruit and leaves, but is very difficult to kill. Reproduction is performed by stakes 20 to 40 inches (50 cm to 1 m) in length obtained from old and vigorous branches, stuck directly into the ground, although in smaller industrial crops advantageously treated cuttings are used. Then they are improved by grafts. The best known table varieties are manzanilla and gordal, and for oil production, Picual, Arbequina, hojiblanca, picudo, and cornicabra.

The grape vine is one of the oldest plants used by humans. This is a bush that has a root, a stalk, and what we call vine shoots, which grow vigorously every spring and where the grape bunches form that so often decorate trellises and shade gardeners as they sit and watch their plants grow.

Vines grow on lattices and cover the tops of pergolas and trellises.

Choose a variety that can climb if you want to have grapes in autumn.

Herbs and

Spices

A corner dedicated to
herbs and spices

Aromatic and culinary herbs are not demanding; you can even have them on a windowsill, and they are a joy for the senses.

The majority of spices, aromatic plants, and medicinal plants can be grown in very little space, even on a little balcony, which is ideal for our garden.

Light

These types of plants generally need a lot of light, so they should be in places where there are no trees in the garden, or if it is a balcony, as close to the railing as possible, or even hung over it in pots. They also like walls that face the sun, like rose bushes do, and you can even have them on a sunny windowsill.

Water

Although they are very hardy plants and many can survive with rainwater alone—like thyme, rosemary, lavender, oregano, fennel—if they are planted in pots they will need abundant watering because the sun dries the soil very quickly. Some, like rosemary and thyme, can tolerate a week of strong sun, while others, like sage and mint, need daily watering at sunrise and sunset.

Fertilizer and mulch

Herbs and spices should not be fertilized too much because our main goal is to keep their aroma and flavor.

It is best to keep the ground free of weeds, and for this, the best option is mulch, which for herbs could be gravel or pine bark.

Pruning

Once they have flowered, remove the dry flowers and trim the plant all over so that it grows new sprouts. If you let the plant grow too much, it will look like it's bolted and will be less pretty and weaker. Another thing is to take the points off the central branches so that they grow to the side and develop a round shape.

A small space

Select your favorite plants. The most common are rosemary, which grows very well with **lavender; thyme**, which is drier and does not need much water; **oregano, sage**, and **marjoram**, which can all share a pot. In another pot you can put **mint** or **spearmint**, **basil**, and **parsley**, which need more water. In any case, after a year you will have to trim the plants well.

Many herbs grow wild in the mountains. Thyme, for example, grows in dry terrain in mild climates, but you will also find rosemary, lavender, oregano . . .

Edible
flowers

Some useful facts about edible flowers

Sometimes we are not aware that although gardens, meadows, and forests can be a source of food, you should get to know them well before consuming anything from them.

Flowering plants—commonly called flowers—are not only an aesthetic element of the first order, which also provide a wonderful fragrance to our garden, but also attract beneficial insects, and, last but not least, give us their flowers as food.

The consumption of flowers is an established custom in the East. In the West, where it is starting to develop, nurseries can already be found in countries such as Spain, France, or Brazil.

Beware that not all flowers can be eaten and many are toxic, so be attentive and well informed. The information on the following pages serve as recommendations, but please consult an expert if you're unsure as to which parts or species of flowers can be consumed.

With flowers (and we do not mean cauliflowers) we only eat the petals. Some violets are eaten whole; however, remove the pistil from most of them, as well as the little white fraction at the base of the petals, which is bitter. They can be eaten raw, in salads, but also in the form of soup or batter, such as squash flowers. Of course, if you are eating the flowers, you should not use any chemicals to kill insects. You must treat them with natural products recommended in this book. Also, weeds must be removed by hand.

Artichoke is an edible flower, but setting it aside as one of our favorites of the garden, the most accessible one is the squash flower.

Squash flowers can be prepared in many ways. Among the most delicious recipes you can find the ones stuffed with monkfish and prawns, or with meat and vegetables, or with fried cheese, accompanied by noodles and shrimp or a rich salad.

A non-exhaustive list of edible flowers:

Borage (*Borago officinalis*)
Flower, preferably blue—but also pink or white—is eaten raw in salads or in ice cubes for cocktails.

Gourds and Squash
Their flowers, bright yellow in color and very large and fleshy, are eaten cooked in stews or soups, but mostly fried with egg and flour batter.

Common daisy (*Bellis perennis*)
It flowers all year round and is eaten raw in salads.

Field marigold (*Calendula arvensis*)
It flowers in winter and spring for very long periods. It is used as a healing ointment. From its orange flowers, sometimes used as a colorant in place of saffron in rice and soups, petals are separated (the center is **not** edible) and added to salads or desserts and even yogurt.

Carnations and pinks
It belongs to the family *Dianthus*; their bright petals are used in salads and creams.

Chrysanthemums (*Chrys. x morifollium*) Belonging to the *Dendranthema* family, it blooms in autumn and the petals are eaten raw in salads and with oranges, but beware against abusing them, because they can be dangerous.

Aztec marigold or Tagetes (*Tagetes erecta*)

Bloom in summer, in full sun; remove the white parts and eat the colored part, especially for rice. In the garden it is a healing plant and neutralizes nematodes.

Hemerocallis or daylily

From the asphodel family, are common in Asia, are grown in full sun and flower throughout the warm season; the flowers are consumed whole, in stews or soups, and roots (raw) and young sprouts (cooked).

Spring or cowslip (*Primula spp.*)

In northern Spain it is yellow if it grows wild, but is also dark blue, purple, or light blue. As the name suggests, it blooms in spring, although it is perennial, and consumed in salads.

Pansy (*Viola vittrockiana*)

It is used in salads and desserts and has diuretic properties.

Chamomile (*Matricaria recutita*)

Or feverfew. It is grown for its flowers when dried to make teas, for its calming and digestive properties, and essential oils for their aroma. Its petals, whose collection requires a great deal of patience, can be eaten in salads.

Rose (*Rosa spp.*)

Its petals are used in baking, for syrups, jams, and marmalades, and rose water is very good for the skin.

Tulip (*Tulipa spp.*)

Petals, of any color, are eaten in salads to which you can add tuna or boiled potatoes

Top: Stuffed endive leaves with marigold petals.
Bottom: Not a bad idea to combine rose petals and pansies.

to give more substance.

Garden nasturtium (*Tropaeolum majus*)

Its orange petals, somewhat spicy, are eaten in salads or cheese.

Violet (*Viola arvensis*)

Blooming in spring, violet or white and everything in between them, their petals are eaten raw and are used to make liquor.

If you dare, try orchid flowers, bougainvillea, chives, nasturtium, sunflowers, geraniums, daisies, yucca flower (big and white), amaranth, lemon, papaya, and orange. But keep away from lilies (of which *only* the bulb is eaten) especially tiger lilies (*Lilium lancifolium*); violas (eat leaves and buttons); Christ thorn; and the poinsettia.

Recipes with flowers

- Chrysanthemums or gladioli salads.
- Pansy jello.
- Thyme flower ice cream with candied violets.
- Jasmine, hollyhock, chamomile, or lavender ice cream.
- Rose petal jam.
- Zucchini flowers with mozzarella and anchovies.
- Flower butter.
- Hollyhock soup.
- Marigold or rose petal omelets. To make the last one, the petals are crushed and mixed with cheeses in portions; add well beaten eggs with salt and place directly in the pan with a little oil.

Never eat flowers bought from a florist

They contain all sorts of chemicals and preservatives added to the water for maintenance. **Ideally, consume your own, but if you want to buy them you must do so in a greenhouse or in a place where they are sold** in pots for planting in the garden itself.

Poisonous Plants

The rediscovery of the benefits of medicinal plants in herbal medicine has led to some abuses. Therefore, in some countries, there is legislation to regulate their consumption. The prohibition of a number of plants and their preparations on the basis of their toxicity and their possible poisonous or narcotic action seems logical: its use for the development and commercialization of pharmaceutical specialties, master formulas, officinal preparations, homeopathic stocks, and research is restricted. The following is a list of some of these toxic plants, organized by toxic syndrome, as per the United States Department of Agriculture.

Abortifacient and Reproductive Toxins
Ponderosa Pine Needles (*Pinus ponderosa*)
Broom Snakeweed (*Gutierrezia sarothrae, microcephala*)

Cardiac Glycoside-Containing Plants
Hemp Dogbane (*Apocynum cannabinum*)

Cyanide or Prussic Acid-Containing Plants
Arrowgrass (*Triglochin spp.*)
Chokecherry (*Prunus spp.*)

Gastrointestinal Irritants and Toxins
Bitterweed (*Hymenoxys odorata*)
Colorado Rubberweed or Pingue (*Hymenoxys richardsoni*)
Sneezeweed (*Helenium hoopesii*)
Copperweed (*Oxytenia acerosa*)

Hepatotoxic and Pyrrolizidine Alkaloid-Containing Plants
Groundsel (*Senecio riddellii,S. longilobus*)
Tansy Ragwort (*Senecio jacobaea*)
Horsebrush (*Tetradymia glabrata, T. canescens*)

Neurotoxic and Myotoxic Plants
Deathcamas (*Zigadenus spp.*)
Larkspur (*Delphinium spp.*)
Locoweed (*Astragalus, Oxytropis spp.*)
Selenium Accumulators (*Astragalus spp.*)
Milkvetch (*Astragalus spp.*)
Rayless Goldenrod (*Haplopappus heterophyllus*)
Lupine (*Lupinus spp.*)

Poison-hemlock (*Conium maculatum*)
Water Hemlock (*Cicuta douglasii*)
Western False Hellebore (*Veratrum californicum*)

Nitrate-Accumulating Plants
Crops such as oat hay, sorghum, corn, sudangrass, Johnsongrass, beets, and weeds such as carelessweed, kochia, pigweed, Russian thistle, and nightshade, are examples of plants that accumulate nitrate. There are many more.

Oxalate-Containing Plants
Greasewood (*Sarcobatus vermiculatus*)
Halogeton (*Halogeton glomeratus*)

Photosensitizing Plants

St. Johnswort (*Hypericum perforatum*)
Spring Parsley (*Cymopterus watsonii*)

Miscellaneous Poisonous Plants
Bracken Fern (*Pteridium aquilinum*)
Oak (*Quercus spp.*)
Other Toxic Plants: Cocklebur (*Xanthium strumarium*), Desert baileya (*Baileya multiradiata*), Drymary or inkweed (*Drymaria pachyphylla*, Horsetail (*Equisetum spp.*), Jimsonweed or thornapple (*Daturaspp.*), Tansy mustard (*Descurainia pinnata*), Yellow star thistle (*Centaurea solstitialis*)
Yew (*Taxus spp.*)

Above: The whole plant *Nierembergia veitchii* is very toxic.
Right, top: *Papaver somniferum* or opium poppy.
Right, below: In the *Magnolia officinalis*, the whole plant is also very toxic.

Above: Hellebore or Christmas rose is a violent purgative and toxic to the heart.
On these lines: Ipomoea violacea L. or black Bodo, whose seeds were used by the Nahuatl of Latin America as hallucinogens.

Above: Lily of the valley causes a disease of the same name that begins to manifest with blurred vision.
Below: The laburnum is a dangerously toxic medicinal plant.

Index

Energy and agriculture

● DOMINGO, J. *Aplicaciones de energías renovables*. Permacultura Montsant. Cornudella. (*Applications of Renewable Energy*)

Commercialization, consumption, quality

● GLÖCKLER, M.; Bockemühl, J.; Tesson, M.F. (1993). *La calidad de los alimentos*. Cuadernos Demeter. Tordera. (*Quality of Foods*)

● LEGASA LABURU, A.M. (1993). *Certificación y comercialización de productos de agricultura ecológica*. Monográficos Bio-Lur. Asociación Bio-Lur Navarra. Tafalla. (*Certification and Commercialization of Ecological Agricultural Products*)

Other subjects

● AKIZU, X.; GARDOKI, M. *Viaje por nueve granjas ecológicas junto al lago Constanza*. Asociación de Agricultura Biodinámica de España. Madrid. (*A Journey Through Nine Ecological Farms Near Lake Constanza*)

● LIEVEGOED, B. C. J. *Las acciones de los planetas y los procesos vitales en el ser humano y en la tierra*. Asociación Biodinámica de España. Madrid. (*The Actions of the Planets on Vital Processes in Human Beings and the Earth*)

● MOLLISON, B. *El agua en permacultura*. Permacultura Montsant. Cornudella. (*Water in Permaculture*)

● VISIONS, D. *Temas claves sobre sostenibilidad*. Permacultura Montsant. Cornudella. (*Key Themes in Sustainability*)

● WISTINGHAUSEN, C.; Scheibe, W. (1996). *Indicaciones para la elaboración de los preparados biodinámicos*. Ed. Rudolf Steiner. Madrid. (*Guide to the Making of Biodynamic Preparations*)

● Ministerio de Medio Ambiente. *Desarrollo de un sistema de identificación/clasificación de peligrosos para el medio ambiente terrestre. Posición y aportaciones españolas en la Unión Europea*. Mundi-Prensa Libros, S.A. Madrid. (*Development of a System of Identification and Classification of Dangers for the Environment. Spanish Position and Contributions to the European Union.*)

Publications

● *Ecoagricultura* Editor: Coordinadora de Agricultura Ecológica (CAE). Address: Apdo. Correos nº 2580. E-08080 Barcelona. Language: Catalán. (*Ecoagriculture*)

● *Ecology and Farming. The International IFOAM Magazine* Editor: IFOAM. Address: Ökozentrum Imsbach. D-66636 Thorley-Theley, Alemania. Language: English www.ecoweb.dk/ifoam/pub/index.aspl

● *Les quatre saisons du jardinage* Editor: Asociación Terre Vivante. Address: Domaine de Raud. F-38710 Mens, Francia. Language: French

● *Permaculture International Journal* Editor: Permaculture International Lt Language: English. www.nor.com.au/environment/perma/data/pij.aspl

● *Permaculture Magazine* Address: Hyden House Limited. Little Hyden Lane. Clanfield. Hampshire. PO8 0RU. England. Language: English. www.gaia.org/permaculture/cover.aspl

● *Savia. Revista de Agricultura Ecológica* Editor: Federación de Agricultura Ecológica FANEGA. Address: Apdo. correos nº 10. E-31300 Tafalla. Tel y fax 948 75 54 04. Language: Spanish. (*Sage. Magazine of Ecological Agriculture*)

Articles, papers, etc.

● *Documentación Primeras Jornadas de Agricultura Ecológica*. (1993). ADAE - SPUPV (*Documentation of the First Seasons of Ecological Agriculture*)

● *Prácticas ecológicas para una agricultura de calidad. Actas del I Congreso de la S.E.A.E.* (1994). SEAE. Toledo. (Ecological Practices for Quality Agriculture: Acts of the First SEAE Congress)

● Ponencias de los cursos de la Escola Agrària de Manresa. (www.visca.com/esagrari/ponenc-c.aspl Email: esagrari@minorisca.es (Course Presentations from the Agrarian School of Manresa)

Connections with other libraries

● Biblioteca de Eco-agro. (Eco-agro Library) www.arrakis.es/~ecoagro/bibliografia.asp

● Permanent Publications Earth Repair Catalogue. www.permaculture.co.uk/menu.asp

● Publicacións do IFOAM. (Publications of the IFOAM) www.ecoweb.dk/ifoam/pub/index.aspl

● Publicacións do Departamento de Agricultura Ecológica da Universidade de Kassel (En Alemán) www.fserv.wiz.unikassel.de/foel/Publicat.aspl (Publications of the Department of Ecological Agriculture of the University of Kassel (In German))

Publishing houses and distributors

● Asociación Vida Sana. Àngel Guimerà, 1, 1º 2ª - 08172 Sant Cugat (Barcelona). Tel. 93 580 08 18. www.vidasana.org

● Can Ricastell (Demeter en España; Asociac. Biodinámica de España). Can Ricastell. 08399 Tordera (Barcelona). Tel: 93 765 03 80. Fax: 93 764 17 84.

● Junta de Extremadura, Address General de Investigación, Producción y Capacitación Agraria. C/ San Vicente, 3 (Apdo. Correos nº 217). 06071 Badajoz.

● Permacultura Montsant C/ Nou, 6. 43360 Cornudella (Tarragona).

● Savia. Apdo. Correos 10. 31300 Tafalla. Tel. y fax 948 75 54 04. Pódese a Savia tanto a revista do mesmo nome coma os monográficos de Bio-Lur Navarra.

● Terapión. C/ Médico Esteve, 2. 46007 Valencia. Tel.: (96) 380 67 67. Fax: (96) 380 86 95.

● Mundi-Prensa Libros. Castelló 37 - 28001 Madrid Tf: 914363700 E-mail: librería@mundiprensa.es Consell de Cent, 391 - 08009 Barcelona Tf: 934883492. E-mail: barcelona@mundiprensa.es www.mundiprensa.com